BAPTISTWAYPRESS®

Adult Bible Study Guide

The Gospel of John

The Word Became Flesh

Duane Brooks

Kay Ellis

Albert Reyes

BAPTISTWAYPRESS®

Dallas, Texas

The Gospel of John: The Word Became Flesh—Adult Bible Study Guide

Copyright © 2006 by BAPTISTWAY PRESS®.
All rights reserved.
Printed in the United States of America.

No part of this book may be used or reproduced in any manner whatsoever without written permission except in the case of brief quotations. For information, contact BAPTISTWAY PRESS, Baptist General Convention of Texas, 333 North Washington, Dallas, TX 75246–1798.

BAPTISTWAY PRESS® is registered in U.S. Patent and Trademark Office.

Scripture marked NIV is taken from The Holy Bible, New International Version (North American Edition), copyright © 1973, 1978, 1984 by the International Bible Society. Used by permission of Zondervan Publishing House. Unless otherwise indicated, all Scripture quotations in unit 1, lessons 1–6; unit 3, lessons 11–13; and the Christmas lesson are from the New International Version.

Scripture marked NASB is taken from the New American Standard Bible®, Copyright © The Lockman Foundation 1960, 1962, 1963, 1968, 1971, 1972, 1973, 1975, 1977, 1995. Used by permission. Unless otherwise indicated, all Scripture quotations in unit 2, lessons 7–10, are from the New American Standard Bible®.

Scripture marked NRSV is taken from the New Revised Standard Version Bible, copyright 1989, Division of Christian Education of the National Council of the Churches of Christ in the United States of America. Used by permission. All rights reserved. Unless otherwise indicated, all Scripture quotations in "Introducing the Gospel of John: The Word Became Flesh" and in the comments on the back cover are from the New Revised Standard Version Bible. The titles of lessons 11–13 are also from the New Revised Standard Version Bible.

BAPTISTWAY PRESS® Management Team
Executive Director, Baptist General Convention of Texas: Charles Wade
Director, Missions, Evangelism, and Ministry Team: Wayne Shuffield
Ministry Team Leader: Phil Miller

Editor & publishing consultant: Ross West, Positive Difference Communications
Cover and Interior Design and Production: Desktop Miracles, Inc.
Printing: Data Reproductions Corporation
Cover Photo: Garden of Gethsemane, istockphoto.com

First edition: December 2006
ISBN: 1–931060–82–7

How to Make the Best Use of This Issue

Whether you're the teacher or a student—

1. Start early in the week before your class meets.
2. Overview the study. Review the table of contents and read the study introduction. Try to see how each lesson relates to the overall study.
3. Use your Bible to read and consider prayerfully the Scripture passages for the lesson. (You'll see that each writer has chosen a favorite translation for the lessons in this issue. You're free to use the Bible translation you prefer and compare it with the translation chosen for that unit, of course.)
4. After reading all the Scripture passages in your Bible, then read the writer's comments. The comments are intended to be an aid to your study of the Bible.
5. Read the small articles—"sidebars"—in each lesson. They are intended to provide additional, enrichment information and inspiration and to encourage thought and application.
6. Try to answer for yourself the questions included in each lesson. They're intended to encourage further thought and application, and they can also be used in the class session itself.

If you're the teacher—

A. Do all of the things just mentioned, of course. In the first session of the study, briefly overview the study by identifying with your class the date on which each lesson will be studied. Lead your class to write the date in the table of contents on page 5 and on the first page of each lesson. You might also find it helpful to make and post a chart that indicates the date on which each lesson will be studied. If all of your class has e-mail, send them an e-mail with the dates the lessons will be studied. (At least one church that uses BAPTISTWAY® materials for its classes places a sticker on the table of contents to identify the dates.) **Note:** A Christmas lesson is included. If your class uses the Christmas lesson, you may need to decide how to study the other lessons, such as by combining two lessons or studying the missed lesson at a special class meeting.
B. Get a copy of the *Teaching Guide*, a companion piece to this *Study Guide*. The *Teaching Guide* contains additional Bible comments plus

two teaching plans. The teaching plans in the *Teaching Guide* are intended to provide practical, easy-to-use teaching suggestions that will work in your class.

C. After you've studied the Bible passage, the lesson comments, and other material, use the teaching suggestions in the *Teaching Guide* to help you develop your plan for leading your class in studying each lesson.

D. You may want to get the additional adult Bible study comments— *Adult Online Bible Commentary*—by Dr. Jim Denison, pastor of Park Cities Baptist Church, Dallas, Texas, that are available at www. baptistwaypress.org and can be downloaded free. An additional teaching plan plus teaching resource items are also available at www.baptistwaypress.org.

E. You also may want to get the enrichment teaching help that is provided on the internet by the *Baptist Standard* at www. baptiststandard.com. (Other class participants may find this information helpful, too.) Call 214–630–4571 to begin your subscription to the printed edition of the *Baptist Standard*.

F. Enjoy leading your class in discovering the meaning of the Scripture passages and in applying these passages to their lives.

Writers of This Study Guide

Duane Brooks, pastor of Tallowood Baptist Church, Houston, Texas, wrote unit one, lessons one through six. Dr. Brooks has been a member of the Executive Board and the Human Welfare Board of the Baptist General Convention of Texas and also a member of the Board of Regents of Baylor University. He has written two previous assignments for BAPTISTWAY®.

Kay Word Ellis wrote unit two, lessons seven through ten. She has Master of Divinity and Master of Theology degrees from Southwestern Baptist Theological Seminary. Kay and her husband are members of Travis Avenue Baptist Church, Fort Worth, Texas. She works as a health coach and freelance writer while caring for her children, Brandon and Katie.

Albert Reyes is the writer of unit three, lessons eleven through thirteen, plus the Christmas lesson. Dr. Reyes is president of Baptist University of the Americas, San Antonio, Texas. He also has served as pastor of churches in Dallas and El Paso. He is a graduate of Angelo State University (B.B.A.) and Southwestern Baptist Theological Seminary (M.Div., D.Min.). He has written three previous assignments for BAPTISTWAY®.

The Gospel of John: The Word Became Flesh

U N I T   O N E

Prologue and Jesus' Public Ministry

Date of Study

U N I T   T W O

Jesus' Farewell Message to His Disciples

THE GOSPEL OF JOHN:
The Word Became Flesh

The Gospel of John is without doubt many people's favorite book of the Bible. Something about its content or the way it approaches its subject attracts people and elevates their perception of this book.

Why This Gospel Is Esteemed So Highly

This Gospel certainly contains many favorite Scripture passages, including passages not found in the other Gospels. Among these favorite passages would be Jesus turning the water into wine (John 2); Jesus conversing with Nicodemus, including perhaps the most quoted verse in all the Bible (John 3; see 3:16); Jesus talking with the Samaritan woman (John 4); Jesus raising Lazarus from the dead (John 11); Jesus instructing and praying for his disciples on the night before his crucifixion (John 13—17). Other similar passages could be named.

In addition, likely another reason the Gospel of John is held in such high esteem is the picture it provides us of Jesus. Of course, each of the four Gospels paints its own unique and valuable portrait of Jesus.[1] In its own unique way, though, the Gospel of John focuses especially on Jesus as God incarnate. This focus is apparent from the first chapter to the last, in incident after incident and teaching after teaching.

The Gospel of John begins not with Jesus' birth (as in Matthew and Luke) or with the beginning of Jesus' ministry (as in Mark). Rather, the Gospel of John begins in the farthest reaches of eternity—even before then, in fact, if we time-bound human beings could even begin to conceive of such a thing. The first verse states, "In the beginning was the Word, and the Word was with God, and the Word was God" (John 1:1).[2] John's Gospel quickly moves to state the mystery of all mysteries and miracle of all miracles, "And the Word became flesh and lived among us, and

9

we have seen his glory. . . " (1:14). Who was this Word? In the very next verse, John the Baptist identifies him without naming him. We do not have to read far to find the name, though. It is *Jesus* (1:29–30).

John's Testimony and Our Choice

Throughout the rest of John's Gospel, this truth of the Word made flesh in Jesus of Nazareth is vividly portrayed. Then, near the end of the Gospel the statement is made, "Now Jesus did many other signs in the presence of his disciples, which are not written in this book. But these are written so that you may come to believe that Jesus is the Messiah, the Son of God, and through believing you may have life in his name" (20:30–31). Finally, the very last verse of the Gospel states, "But there are also many other things that Jesus did; if every one of them were written down, I suppose that the world itself could not contain the books that would be written" (21:25). These three verses in the closing chapters of the Gospel of John seem to say that although adequate witness to lead to belief in Jesus as the incarnate Word has been given in this Gospel, even more could be provided.

So, from the beginning to the end of the Gospel of John, we are left with this testimony—and a choice. As C.S. Lewis (1898–1963), the British writer and Christian thinker, wrote decades ago in a book that has continued to remain on the best-seller list: "Either this man was, and is, the Son of God: or else a madman or something worse. You can shut Him up for a fool, you can spit at Him and kill Him as a demon; or you can fall at His feet and call Him Lord and God. But let us not come with any patronising nonsense about His being a great human teacher. He has not left that open to us. He did not intend to."[3] Neither does the Gospel of John.

Studying This Gospel

If you were to read the Gospel of John at one sitting, which you may want to do in preparation for this study, you would see that John 1—12 tells us of Jesus' life up until the beginning of the final week. Then you would see that John 13—17 portrays events on the night before Jesus' crucifixion.

Finally, you would see that John 18—21 pictures Jesus' arrest, trial, crucifixion, and resurrection appearances.

That is how we will study this Gospel. Unit one contains six lessons from the first portion, dealing with the prologue and Jesus' public ministry, with lessons from John 1, 3, 4, 5, 6, and 11. Unit two provides studies on John 13—17, Jesus' farewell messages to his disciples and his prayer for them. Unit three offers guidance in studying John 18—21, on Jesus' crucifixion and resurrection.

Note: The time of the first release of these materials includes the Christmas holiday. To meet the needs of churches who wish to have an emphasis on Christmas at this time, a Christmas lesson is included.

Additional Resources for Studying the Gospel of John[4]

George R. Beasley-Murray. *John*. Word Biblical Commentary. Volume 36. Waco, Texas: Word Books, Publisher, 1987.

Raymond E. Brown. *The Gospel According to John (I—XII)*. Garden City, New York: Doubleday & Company, Inc., 1966.

Raymond E. Brown. *The Gospel According to John (XIII—XXI)*. Garden City, New York: Doubleday & Company, Inc., 1970.

F.F. Bruce. *The Gospel of John*. Grand Rapids, Michigan: William B. Eerdmans Publishing Company, 1983.

Gary M. Burge, *The NIV Application Commentary: John*. Grand Rapids, Michigan: Zondervan Publishing House, 2000.

D. A. Carson, *The Farewell Discourse and Final Prayer of Jesus*. Grand Rapids, Michigan: Baker Book House, 1980.

James E. Carter. *John*. Layman's Bible Book Commentary. Volume 18. Nashville: Broadman Press, 1984.

Herschel H. Hobbs. *The Gospel of John: Invitation to Life*. Nashville, Tennessee: Convention Press, 1988.

William E. Hull. "John." *The Broadman Bible Commentary*. Volume 9. Nashville, Tennessee: Broadman Press, 1970.

Craig S. Keener. *The Gospel of John: A Commentary*. Two volumes. Peabody, Massachusetts: Hendrickson Publishers, 2003.

Lesslie Newbigin. *The Light Has Come: An Exposition of the Fourth Gospel*. Grand Rapids, Michigan: William B. Eerdmans Publishing Company, 1982.

Gail R. O'Day. "The Gospel of John." *The New Interpreter's Bible*. Volume IX. Nashville, Tennessee: Abingdon Press, 1995.

NOTES

1. Although Matthew, Mark, and Luke are called the *synoptic* Gospels, meaning that they tend to "see together" on the story of Jesus, each of them approaches this story in its own unique way, even so.
2. Unless otherwise indicated, all Scripture quotations in this article are from the New Revised Standard Version.
3. C.S. Lewis, *Mere Christianity* (New York: HarperSanFrancisco, 2000 [originally published in 1952]), 52.
4. Listing a book does not imply full agreement by the writers or BAPTISTWAY PRESS® with all of its comments.

Prologue and Jesus' Public Ministry

Unit one, "Prologue and Jesus' Public Ministry," consists of six lessons on John 1—11. The unit begins with a study of what is known as the *prologue* (John 1:1–18). The prologue introduces the entire Gospel of John and points to its meaning. The next five lessons are on Jesus' conversation with Nicodemus (John 3); Jesus' conversation with the Samaritan woman (John 4); Jesus' healing of the lame man (John 5); Jesus' feeding the 5,000 (John 6); and Jesus' raising of Lazarus (John 11).[1]

UNIT ONE. PROLOGUE AND JESUS' PUBLIC MINISTRY

Lesson 1	From Eternity to Here	John 1:1–18, 29–36, 43–45
Lesson 2	Searching for Real Life	John 3:1–16
Lesson 3	Meeting the Savior of the World	John 4:1–30, 39–42
Lesson 4	Honoring the Son	John 5:1–24
Lesson 5	Relying On Our Only Hope	John 6:1–15, 25–35, 48–51, 66–69
Lesson 6	Believing in Jesus as the Resurrection and the Life	John 11:1–13, 17–27, 38–44

NOTES

1. Unless otherwise indicated, all Scripture quotations in this unit introduction and lessons 1–6 are from the New International Version.

Focal Text

John 1:1–18, 29–36, 43–45

Background

John 1

Main Idea

We are called to follow Jesus in light of the magnificent truth that the God of eternity came to live among us in him.

Question to Explore

Why follow the man named Jesus?

Study Aim

To describe how the eternal God became incarnate and made himself known in Jesus and state how this is to affect our lives today

Study and Action Emphases

- Affirm the Bible as our authoritative guide for life and ministry
- Share the gospel with all people
- Obey and serve Jesus by meeting physical, spiritual, and emotional needs

LESSON ONE

From Eternity to Here

Quick Read

Nothing would justify Jesus' journey from eternity to now other than this: the Creator became a child so that we his creation might become his children by following Jesus.

Jesus made the list! A recent survey of the world's most admired people revealed that Jesus made the top ten list. Ironically, he did not come in first place. It is hard to imagine a list of great people in which Jesus would not lead the parade.

What would Jesus think about his slide on the popularity charts? Actually, Jesus never came to attract admirers; he was looking for followers.

John began his story of Jesus and his followers with a powerful prologue showing that Jesus, the eternal Word, was the Creator God before the foundation of the world. The Gospel of Matthew tells us the story of Jesus' entrance into the world from Joseph's vantage point. The Gospel of Luke opens Mary's treasure box of memories for us. But the Gospel of John goes back further than the beginning of time, to the time when there was no time. The Gospel of John describes Jesus' journey from eternity to a world of days and years, minutes and seconds.

John 1:1–18, 29–36, 43–45

[1]In the beginning was the Word, and the Word was with God, and the Word was God. [2]He was with God in the beginning.

[3]Through him all things were made; without him nothing was made that has been made. [4]In him was life, and that life was the light of men. [5]The light shines in the darkness, but the darkness has not understood it.

[6]There came a man who was sent from God; his name was John. [7]He came as a witness to testify concerning that light, so that through him all men might believe. [8]He himself was not the light; he came only as a witness to the light. [9]The true light that gives light to every man was coming into the world.

[10]He was in the world, and though the world was made through him, the world did not recognize him. [11]He came to that which was his own, but his own did not receive him. [12]Yet to all who received him, to those who believed in his name, he gave the right to become children of God—[13]children born not of natural descent, nor of human decision or a husband's will, but born of God.

[14]The Word became flesh and made his dwelling among us. We have seen his glory, the glory of the One and Only, who came from the Father, full of grace and truth.

[15]John testifies concerning him. He cries out, saying, "This was he of whom I said, 'He who comes after me has surpassed me because he was before me.'" [16]From the fullness of his grace we have all received one

blessing after another. [17]For the law was given through Moses; grace and truth came through Jesus Christ. [18]No one has ever seen God, but God the One and Only, who is at the Father's side, has made him known.

. . . .

[29]The next day John saw Jesus coming toward him and said, "Look, the Lamb of God, who takes away the sin of the world! [30]This is the one I meant when I said, 'A man who comes after me has surpassed me because he was before me.' [31]I myself did not know him, but the reason I came baptizing with water was that he might be revealed to Israel."

[32]Then John gave this testimony: "I saw the Spirit come down from heaven as a dove and remain on him. [33]I would not have known him, except that the one who sent me to baptize with water told me, 'The man on whom you see the Spirit come down and remain is he who will baptize with the Holy Spirit.'[34] I have seen and I testify that this is the Son of God."

[35]The next day John was there again with two of his disciples. [36]When he saw Jesus passing by, he said, "Look, the Lamb of God!"

. . . .

[43]The next day Jesus decided to leave for Galilee. Finding Philip, he said to him, "Follow me."

[44]Philip, like Andrew and Peter, was from the town of Bethsaida. [45]Philip found Nathanael and told him, "We have found the one Moses wrote about in the Law, and about whom the prophets also wrote—Jesus of Nazareth, the son of Joseph."

The Word, Life, and Light (1:1–9)

The Gospel of John evokes powerful thoughts and emotions with its depictions of Jesus. Jesus is the Word, the life, and the light. We find in this Gospel a marvelous portrait of a Jesus who was both completely human and fully divine.

In the first-century world, many would have acknowledged that Jesus was a great prophet. Some of these would have seen John the Baptist as Jesus' equal or even as his superior. So the Gospel of John tells the truth about Jesus so that all would know him as the only answer.

The world sometimes asks, *If Jesus is the answer, what is the question?* The Gospel of John responds, *Whatever the question, Jesus is the answer.*

Jesus existed before time as God. He was with God, and he was God. More than a mere human being who appeared on earth in the first century, Jesus was God before the foundation of the world.

Jesus, as the *Logos*, created the world (John 1:1–3, 10–18). His work of creation was comprehensive and complete. "Through him all things were made. Without him nothing was made that has been made" (1:3). These words sound in harmony with Paul's writings and the Letter to the Hebrews. In Colossians 1:16, Paul tells us that "all things were created by him and for him." Similarly, the writer of Hebrews penned in his prologue, "In these last days God has spoken to us by his Son . . . through whom he made the universe" (Hebrews 1:2).

> *Jesus never came to attract admirers; he was looking for followers.*

As the "light," Jesus illumines the world. We hear echoes of Isaiah 60—61 in John's words. For John "the world" was not just the created universe, but that universe as fallen and in direct opposition to God. The world can be a dark place. Later Jesus said on the occasion of healing the man born blind in John 9:4, "As long as it is day, we must do the work of him who sent me. Night is coming, when no one can work." In John 5:35, we learn that John the Baptist was a "lamp," but, in 9:5, Jesus declares, "As long as I am in the world, I am the light of the world" (NRSV).

In the Gospel of John we discover immediately that something is now desperately wrong with the world. Jesus made the world, but now the world that he made does not recognize him or receive him. The world still belongs to him, but it is now in a desperate attempt to secede from his reign through sin. So in John 1:29, Jesus, the Lamb of God, comes to take away the sin of the world. Later in the Gospel, we learn that followers of Christ "do not belong to the world" (John 15:19), and we learn that in this world we "will have trouble" (16:33). Again, in 18:36, Jesus said, "My kingdom is not of this world." But the Gospel of John shows us in John 3:16 that God loves this world in spite of its flaws and failures.

The Gift Rejected! (1:10–11)

Even in a first-century religious culture that anticipated the Messiah, so many missed the incarnation of God! We must be careful in America's religious milieu not to miss the true identity of Christ. Many in our world

Jesus, John the Baptist, and Moses

In the Fourth Gospel, John the Evangelist traced the relationship of Jesus to two great prophetic figures in the Old and New Testaments. In John 1:8 we learn that John the Baptist was not "the light." In John 1:15, John the Baptist's own words recognize Jesus' superiority: "He who comes after me has surpassed me because he was before me." In the same context, we discover the superiority of Jesus' ministry to Moses' ministry. It is true that Moses brought the law, but Jesus brought "grace and truth" (1:17). John the Baptist explicitly admitted that he was not the Christ (1:20). In another comparison, John the Baptist said in 1:26–27, "I baptize with water, but among you stands one you do not know. He is the one who comes after me, the thongs of whose sandals I am not worthy to untie." Further, Jesus will "baptize with the Holy Spirit," not just with water (1:33).

---

still do not recognize him. "He came to that which was his own, but his own did not receive him" (1:11).

Who were "his own"? Jesus came as a Jew to his own people, but we must understand that we are all "his own." The whole universe belongs to him. Psalm 24:1 reminds us, "The earth is the Lord's and everything in it, the world and all who live in it."

As I returned from lunch at a local barbecue restaurant one day, my assistant asked me, "So how was lunch?"

The Gospel of John describes Jesus' journey from eternity to a world of days and years, minutes and seconds.

"Fine," I said, walking by her desk.

She asked again, "No, really. Did you see him?"

Then it came back to me. Encountering church members there, I had moved into a back dining area. Sitting with my back to the door, I heard a great commotion at one point but continued to converse with my friends. As I left the restaurant, I had noticed a long line of black limousines. I distinctly remember wondering for a moment why they were there, but I moved on to my car without doing anything to satisfy my curiosity. I asked my secretary, "Did I see whom?"

She said, "The forty-first president, George H. W. Bush! You did see him, didn't you? Church members who saw you there told me to ask you about it."

I had been sitting in the same restaurant with the former president and his entourage but was so preoccupied with my own agenda that I had missed it. In the same way, when Jesus, the long-awaited Messiah, came to the world, most of the world didn't even notice. Still others noticed but rejected him outright. Looking for a king, they missed Jesus, who came as a baby. "The Infinite has become an infant," as the great Baptist preacher Charles Spurgeon (1834–1892) wrote,[1] and God's greatest gift experienced rejection.

If Jesus were here physically, would we know him? Most depictions of Jesus are of a blue-eyed, long-haired man with a beard. But would Jesus have been white? Certainly he would have looked like people from the Middle East look. He might have been looked at suspiciously or selectively profiled were he to enter our world today. Mother Teresa ministered to the people in the streets of Calcutta and called the poor "Jesus in distressing disguise."

> We find in this Gospel a marvelous portrait of a Jesus who was both completely human and fully divine.

In a disturbing parable in Matthew 25, Jesus said, "Whatever you did for one of the least of these brothers of mine, you did for me" (Matthew 25:40). We can find Jesus here, if we will look for him in the last, the lost, and the least in our community. He often lives under a bridge.

Receiving Him (1:12–18)

The Gospel of John tells us that those who receive Christ by believing in him receive a relationship that redefines their fundamental identity: "To all who received him, to those who believed in his name, he gave the right to become children of God" (John 1:12)! The parameters of God's grace provide room for all. The way to receive Christ is to believe in his name. The Gospel of John shows us the promise. Jesus gave us the right "to become," to be "born" (1:12–13). To become children of God, we first must be born. This verse portends and prepares for the conversation of Jesus with Nicodemus (John 3). This is not mere physical birth ("born, not of blood or of the will of the flesh or of the will of man, but of God," 1:13, NRSV). Rather it is spiritual birth.

> . . . God loves this world in spite of its flaws and failures.

Many believe and teach that all are children of God by virtue of their creation in God's image. God has certainly created all humankind. But to

Images for Jesus

In this opening chapter, John gives us several stirring images that communicate Jesus' identity: *Word, light, life, Son of God, Lamb of God, King of Israel*. What are other names, images, or titles for Jesus in the Gospels? To which of these do you feel the most connection today? Spend some time worshiping Jesus by reflecting on that truth about who he is.

---

become God's children requires a second birth from above. This spiritual birth is the work of the Holy Spirit through Christ. We are born again when we believe in the "name," or *authority*, of Jesus Christ and become followers of him.

Verse 14 shows us the truth about the incarnation. Jesus was not a man who became God; he was God who became man. He is the only One who is "full of grace and truth"—the only One who can give us life.

The Witness (1:29–36)

In John 1:29 we discover yet another description of Jesus. John the Baptist pointed to the future sacrifice of Christ by calling him "the Lamb of God, who takes away the sin of the world!" As the forerunner to Jesus' ministry, John the Baptist's whole ministry served to facilitate the revelation of Jesus. John rooted his testimony in the authority of the Spirit who came down from heaven "as a dove" and rested on Jesus. Jesus would baptize not with water but

> *We can find Jesus here, if we will look for him in the last, the lost, and the least in our community.*

with this same confirming Spirit. Ultimately, John the Baptist knew he must "become less" so that Jesus could "become greater" (3:30). John the Baptist initiated this process by showing the Lamb to his disciples and sending them after Jesus (1:35–36). These former followers of John the Baptist became the first followers of Christ.

To this day, we find a great deal of competition between ministers and ministries. Often within the church, leaders become possessive of people and resources. John the Baptist becomes a great example to us in this regard. When we realize the primacy of Christ, then we do not seek our own glory or success. We begin to see the growth of other ministries as blessings for God's kingdom, and we rejoice with those who rejoice.

The Way (1:43–45)

Once Andrew and the other disciple had followed Jesus, Andrew found his brother Simon Peter and proclaimed that they had found the Messiah (1:40–41). As Jesus planned to return to Galilee, he called Philip to follow him. Jesus offered this calling—following him—to his disciples.

In a further explanation of Jesus' relationship to Moses, Philip found Nathanael and explained that Jesus was the one about whom Moses wrote in the law. So Moses and the prophets pointed to Jesus. As Jesus invited Andrew and Andrew's friend to "come" and "see" (1:39), Philip invited Nathanael to "come and see" Jesus for himself (1:46). These men became the first disciples of Jesus. Eventually they made other disciples, but first they became disciples themselves.

> *Jesus was not a man who became God; he was God who became man.*

Christ has extended the calling to make disciples to all of his followers. Like these early believers, we tend to make only the kind of disciples that we ourselves are. Are we following Christ, or are we following others? Do we admire Jesus, or will we follow him?

Donald Miller tells in his book *Blue Like Jazz* about a friend of his, Alan, who surveyed leading ministers. Alan's cross-country study included an interview with Dr. Bill Bright, the founder of Campus Crusade for Christ. Alan described Dr. Bright as "a big man, full of life, who listened without shifting his eyes." Alan's final question to Dr. Bright was, *What does Jesus mean to you?* Miller writes, "Alan said Dr. Bright could not answer the question. He said Dr. Bright just started to cry. He sat there in his big chair behind his big desk and wept."[2]

Wouldn't you like to know Jesus like that, with your heart and not just with your head?

22

QUESTIONS

1. Where do you see evidence of the divinity of Christ in this passage? What difference does it make to us that Jesus was fully divine as well as fully human?

2. Are you ever possessive of your ministry within the church? How does John the Baptist's example enlighten this issue for you?

3. The two disciples chose the best over the good when they chose Jesus over John the Baptist. Do you ever settle for the good instead of the best? Prayerfully consider: Is there any area where you have settled for less than God's best?

4. What visible, audible, tangible difference has your commitment to Christ made in your life? in the lives of others?

NOTES

1. Charles Haddon Spurgeon, "Men Made Rich by the Poverty of Christ." See www.bartleby.com.
2. Donald Miller, *Blue Like Jazz* (Nashville, Tennessee: Thomas Nelson, 2003), 233.

Study Aim
To determine how I need to respond to Jesus' insistence on being "born from above"

Study and Action Emphases

- Affirm the Bible as our authoritative guide for life and ministry
- Share the gospel with all people
- Develop a growing, vibrant faith

LESSON TWO

Searching for Real Life

Quick Read
When Nicodemus came to Jesus at night, he discovered that real life comes through faith in the God who loves us and gives us a new spiritual birth.

As I visited with a guest in our church, she revealed that she had been raised as an Orthodox Jew. I also discovered that she was a NASA scientist who had written software that runs in the space shuttle and that she had gotten a perfect 1600 on her SAT. As the conversation progressed, she asked me directly, "Why should I believe in your Messiah?"

I started to explain to her simply, "Well, you don't have to be a rocket scientist . . . " but she *was* a rocket scientist! Suddenly feeling very dumb, I said to her, "I don't know much, but there was this guy named C.S. Lewis. He was very smart, and he wrote a book called *Mere Christianity*." I gave her a copy of that book and a Bible as well.

Before she left, she said, "I have three weeks to get my life together." Three weeks later, she came back, having read the New Testament and *Mere Christianity*. Then she told me the new developments in her story. Before Mother's Day, her dad had died suddenly of a heart attack, and she had had a long conversation with her mom, telling her she was exploring Christianity. Then her mother had told her, "You must give up pursuing other religions." She refused her mom's advice. During the interim between our meetings, her mom had decided that it would be better not to live than to live without her dad and had taken her own life.

So when she came for our next appointment, she was in great grief. She asked again, "Why should I believe in your Messiah?" I told her about Jesus, who said, "Come unto me, all you who are weary and burdened" (Matthew 11:28). She told me if she went public with her faith, her family would disown her. I remember the morning service when she walked down the aisle in front of everybody and received Christ as her Savior.

Early in Jesus' ministry, John tells us he encountered one of the religious *who's who* of his day, a man named Nicodemus who came to him at night. Jesus' ministry affected the entire fabric of Jewish society, including the religious leaders. One of the most prominent religious leaders of that day, Nicodemus, came to Jesus seeking to understand his ministry. The Gospel of John uniquely offers us this insight into the thoughts and actions of one of the religious leaders who were wrestling with the meaning of Jesus' ministry.

A popular Christian band called Switchfoot asks a haunting question in a song many young people know well, "Are you who you want to be?"[1] Nicodemus might have been struggling with that same issue when he sought a nighttime meeting with Jesus. Nicodemus was looking for real life.

Nicodemus may well have been one of the most religious people of his day. First, he worshiped the one living God. Judaism was superior as a religion to the worship of the Roman emperor and the mystery religions of the Greek world. Second, Nicodemus was good at religion. He had advanced within Judaism to become a member of the Sanhedrin, the ruling council.

But for all of his religion, something was missing. Nicodemus was an expert at the rules, but he was missing the relationship. This is why he said to Jesus, "No one could perform the miraculous signs you are doing if God were not with him" (John 3:2). Nicodemus had the form but not the force of true spirituality. He saw power in Jesus' life that was missing in his own.

John 3:1–16

[1] Now there was a man of the Pharisees named Nicodemus, a member of the Jewish ruling council. [2] He came to Jesus at night and said, "Rabbi, we know you are a teacher who has come from God. For no one could perform the miraculous signs you are doing if God were not with him."

[3] In reply Jesus declared, "I tell you the truth, no one can see the kingdom of God unless he is born again."

[4] "How can a man be born when he is old?" Nicodemus asked. "Surely he cannot enter a second time into his mother's womb to be born!"

[5] Jesus answered, "I tell you the truth, no one can enter the kingdom of God unless he is born of water and the Spirit. [6] Flesh gives birth to flesh, but the Spirit gives birth to spirit. [7] You should not be surprised at my saying, 'You must be born again.' [8] The wind blows wherever it pleases. You hear its sound, but you cannot tell where it comes from or where it is going. So it is with everyone born of the Spirit."

[9] "How can this be?" Nicodemus asked.

[10] "You are Israel's teacher," said Jesus, "and do you not understand these things? [11] I tell you the truth, we speak of what we know, and we testify to what we have seen, but still you people do not accept our testimony. [12] I have spoken to you of earthly things and you do not believe; how then will you believe if I speak of heavenly things? [13] No one has ever gone into heaven except the one who came from heaven—the Son of Man. [14] Just as Moses lifted up the snake in the desert, so the Son of Man must be lifted up, [15] that everyone who believes in him may have eternal life.

> [16]"For God so loved the world that he gave his one and only Son, that whoever believes in him shall not perish but have eternal life."

Spiritual Regeneration Begins When We Admit Our Inability to Save Ourselves (3:1–2)

Who was Nicodemus? He was a member of the Jewish ruling council. Jesus used the definite article to say in verse 10 that Nicodemus was *the* teacher of Israel.

Why did Nicodemus come to see Jesus? He was obviously dissatisfied with the way his life was.

Nicodemus came at night, in part to maintain his secrecy (3:2). Remember John 12:42–43: "Yet at the same time many even among the leaders believed in him. But because of the Pharisees they would not confess their faith for fear they would be put out of the synagogue; for they loved praise from men more than praise from God."

Even so, Nicodemus came with a deep recognition of God's presence in Jesus' life. We see this in the terms with which Nicodemus approached Jesus and described him. Nicodemus referred to Jesus as "Rabbi," "teacher," one "who has come from God," and one empowered by God's presence to perform miracles (3:2).

Nicodemus himself was a teacher, but he readily admitted that he did not have Jesus' power in his life. It was a moment of decision for him. We notice Jesus' response in 3:3, but a response to what? Nothing had been asked. But Jesus perceived the question Nicodemus was asking by his presence: *How do I get what you have?* We can never come to God until we come to the end of ourselves. To be born again, Nicodemus had to give up his efforts to save himself.

As the conversation progressed, she asked me directly, "Why should I believe in your Messiah?"

What would we have to give up to be ready for relationship with God? Pharisaism remains alive and well in our world and especially in the church today. What if we gave up our pride in our ethnic group, in our position, in our wealth, in our pretentious piety, and in our judgmental spirit towards others? What if we gave up our mixture of patriotism with religion? What if we repented of our lack of concern for social justice and the needs of people in our world?

28

Nicodemus was religious in the worst sense of the word, especially if we mean by religion the human effort to get to God. The gospel, though, is the story of God coming to bring us to himself!

Spiritual Regeneration Transforms Us into Children of God Through Spiritual Rebirth from Above (3:3–8)

Jesus saw that Nicodemus was searching. Jesus offered him a new way to see. "I tell you the truth, no one can see the kingdom of God unless he is born again" (3:3). Was Jesus saying, *You can't get to heaven unless you are born again?* Yes. But Jesus was also saying more than that: *Not only can you not get to heaven, but also heaven can't get to you.* We cannot build or establish the kingdom of God, but the New Testament teaches that we can "receive" and "enter" it (Matt. 5:20; 7:21; 18:3; 19:23–24; 23:13; Mark 9:47; 10:15). Hebrews 12:28 says, "We are receiving a kingdom." You can't have a kingdom without a king. Wherever Jesus reigns without rival, God's kingdom has already come, if we have eyes to see. The kingdom of God is the very power and work that Nicodemus saw in Jesus. Jesus invited him to receive it through spiritual rebirth.

> Nicodemus was looking for real life.

Summary of John 2

After Jesus called his first disciples, he performed his first miracle, transforming the water into wine at the wedding at Cana. John saw special significance in these miracles, and so he called them *signs.*

After Jesus left Cana, Jesus went to Jerusalem for the first of three Passovers during his ministry. On his entry into the temple, he was deeply troubled by those who were using the temple courts for profit by selling animals and exchanging money. Jesus cleared the temple, scattering money on the ground to demonstrate the comparative worth of the Gentiles' access to God over the material gain. To this day many see Christianity and ministry as an occasion for personal gain, valuing money over people.

Through Jesus' signs, many were coming to profess faith in him. Jesus, though, found his self-understanding not in the speculation of the masses or even of the religious leaders but in his relationship with the heavenly Father.

In verse 3, the words translated "born again" literally mean *born from above*. Jesus told Nicodemus and tells us that we need outside help from above. So this new birth is not by our efforts, energy, or intellect, but by the grace of God (John 1:13). There are some things we cannot do for ourselves. It is all God's work. We cannot try harder to be born, but we can trust God.

Nicodemus misunderstood Jesus' assertion that one must be born from above. He took his words literally to say one must be born again physically. In John 3:4, Nicodemus asked, "How can a man be born when he is old? . . . Surely he cannot enter a second time into his mother's womb to be born." In other words, *How would this work for a person like me? You can't teach an old dog new tricks, you know.*

Nicodemus was religious in the worst sense of the word. . . .

In 1990, my grandfather called me from Washington State and asked me to come and speak with him about the Lord. He suffered the exhausting regimen of kidney dialysis every two days. My father and I met in Portland and drove to my grandfather's home. As I shared with my grandfather, he received Christ and followed the Lord in baptism in a small Baptist church there.

Jesus clarified that those who wish to enter the kingdom of God must be born of water and Spirit. Some take this to mean that one must be born physically and spiritually. Others take it to mean that one must be born of water baptism and the Spirit. We find help in John 3:6: "Flesh gives birth to flesh." We have all been physically born. But only the Spirit gives birth to spirit.

Then Jesus corrected Nicodemus and said, "You should not be surprised at my saying," and again said, "You must be born again" (3:7). He used the analogy of the wind that blows. We hear its sound, but we cannot tell where it comes from or where it is going. Along the Gulf Coast region, many are painfully aware of the unpredictability of the wind. Even the best forecasters cannot predict precisely the landing spot or time of a hurricane. But all can see the effects of it.

What would we have to give up to be ready for relationship with God?

At this point, Nicodemus was totally confused and said (3:9), "How can this be?" Jesus responded (3:10): "You are Israel's teacher . . . and do not understand these things?" Like Nicodemus, we must emerge from the darkness into the light with our commitment to Christ.

30

Spiritual Regeneration Fulfills
God's Plan for Our Lives (3:9–16)

Did Nicodemus become a Christ follower that night? Clearly Nicodemus was fascinated with Jesus. Three times Jesus said, "I tell you the truth" (3:3, 5, 11), and three times he invited Nicodemus to be born again. Then Jesus concluded sadly, in 3:11, "We speak of what we know, and we testify to what we have seen, but still you people do not accept our testimony." Jesus had spoken of earthly things, but Nicodemus did not comprehend him. Now Jesus was speaking of heavenly things.

Nicodemus was an expert at the rules, but he was missing the relationship.

We have all heard that some are so heavenly minded that they are no earthly good. For most of us, this is not really a great concern. What if, on the other hand, we are so earthly minded that we are no heavenly good? Paul later wrote to the Colossians, "Set your minds on things above, not on earthly things" (Colossians 3:2). Jesus can speak accurately and reliably about heaven because it is his permanent mailing address. Jesus has gone to heaven and can speak about it because he came from heaven (John 3:13).

John 3:14 recalls one of the great moments of deliverance, recorded in Numbers 21. After the people of Israel experienced the judgment of their sin through serpents, Moses made a bronze serpent. If the snake-bit people looked up to the serpent, they were spared death. As Moses lifted up the serpent in the desert and people came and were healed, so Jesus must be "lifted up" (as one would be on a cross; see John 12:32) for people to believe in him. It is Jesus' work on the cross that saves us; it is Jesus' work that sanctifies us.

We can be born from above today, if we will receive God's gracious provision of salvation by placing our trust in Jesus Christ.

So John offers the clearest, most succinct, and most beloved summary of the gospel in a single sentence: *God loves people so much that he sent his one and only Son so that whoever believes in him will not perish but have everlasting life.* The world still needs to hear this truth!

Jan was relaxing in the hotel hot tub after the day's sessions at an Athletes in Action evangelism conference. Two adolescent girls also staying at the hotel slipped into the whirlpool as well. One of the teens was clearly excited about an upcoming Wiccan gathering. Jan normally

Being Accessible and Approachable

The encounter between Jesus and Nicodemus was possible because Jesus was known to be accessible and approachable. People knew where they could find him and that he would welcome honest conversation with them when they got there.

Where are places and times in your life, your family, and your church when pre-Christians seeking spiritual truth know that they can find you and have open and affirming dialogue with you? How could you make yourself more available to those who have questions about what it means to follow Jesus?

would have taken this occult deception straight on with some hard-nosed apologetics but felt a prompting from the Spirit to simply listen instead.

When the girls' conversation paused, Jan said "Wow, you really sound excited about this!" That was an invitation for her to hear a five-minute mini-seminar on the attractions and advantages of participating in neo-pagan rituals. But it also uncovered that the girl had had a traumatic high school experience and the Wiccans had accepted her anyway. Still, the girl betrayed her lingering dissatisfaction when she said, "I've gone through so much just trying to make it through high school that I'll probably be in therapy for the rest of my life!"

Jan made an attempt to let her know she had been heard by mirroring back her words of pain, saying, "It's hard for you to even imagine a future where you'd be free from all of the pain you've gone through." The response from the teenager floored Jan. Through welling tears and in a voice stripped of pretense, her new friend said, "Sometimes I wish I could be born all over again. I'd really like to start over from scratch." Because a loving ear took the time to hear, she got the chance to do exactly that.[2]

All of us have longed for a new beginning. That new beginning is found in Jesus Christ alone. We can be born from above today, if we will receive God's gracious provision of salvation by placing our trust in Jesus Christ.

QUESTIONS

1. What do you think was the greatest obstacle to Nicodemus being born again? How do you identify with his struggle in that regard?

2. What does Jesus say in this conversation about how the Holy Spirit is active in giving us new birth? Can you think of other biblical passages that talk about the Spirit's role in salvation?

3. Jesus didn't initially promise Nicodemus a chance to have eternal life but rather to "enter the kingdom of God" (John 3:5)? What is the kingdom of God? Why does Jesus equate entering it with salvation?

4. We do not build or establish the kingdom, but rather we receive it as a gift and enter it as one being born into a new world. How does this affect the way you view following Jesus and his command for us to disciple others to do the same?

5. Nicodemus's story didn't end in John 3 (see 7:50–51; 19:39–41). He continued to search. In John 19 we see him showing allegiance to Jesus. Think about two or three lost friends you have. What stage are they in on their spiritual journeys? How can you, like Jesus, perhaps move your friends one step closer to faith in him?

NOTES

1. "This Is Your Life," lyrics by Jon Foreman.
2. Steve Sjogren, Dave Ping, Doug Pollock, *Irresistible Evangelism* (Loveland, Colorado: Group Publishing, 2003),109.

Focal Text

John 4:1–30, 39–42

Background

John 4:1–42

Main Idea

Jesus offers himself and his way to all who will receive him, whatever their life circumstances.

Question to Explore

How would you explain your life and your views about people if you could talk directly with Jesus?

Study Aim

To trace the meaning of the conversation between Jesus and the Samaritan woman and state its implications for a person's relationship with Jesus

Study and Action Emphases

- Affirm the Bible as our authoritative guide for life and ministry
- Share the gospel with all people
- Develop a growing, vibrant faith
- Include all God's family in decision-making and service
- Value all people as created in the image of God

LESSON THREE

Meeting the Savior of the World

Quick Read

When Jesus kept a divine appointment with a Samaritan woman at the well, she received the living water of eternal life and shared it with her whole city.

"I've been considering Buddhism because of all the suffering in my life." His words wrested my attention away from the book I was reading. On a plane trip, coming home from the holidays with my family, I sat next to a man who told me his life story. I had hoped to read a favorite new book until he began to recount the pain of his past.

Reared in the shadow of the steeple of my congregation, he had endured his parents' divorce when he was ten. Although he held a good job, he struggled with poor health. Numerous surgeries had taken a toll on him. He spoke of how his sister had died of cancer at a young age. A broken relationship had left him feeling alone in the world.

As we talked about Buddhism and its acknowledgment of suffering, I invited him to return to the faith of his childhood, to serve the God who not only sees our suffering, but shared in it through his incarnation and crucifixion.

John 4:1–30, 39–42

¹The Pharisees heard that Jesus was gaining and baptizing more disciples than John, ²although in fact it was not Jesus who baptized, but his disciples. ³When the Lord learned of this, he left Judea and went back once more to Galilee.

⁴Now he had to go through Samaria. ⁵So he came to a town in Samaria called Sychar, near the plot of ground Jacob had given to his son Joseph. ⁶Jacob's well was there, and Jesus, tired as he was from the journey, sat down by the well. It was about the sixth hour.

⁷When a Samaritan woman came to draw water, Jesus said to her, "Will you give me a drink?" ⁸(His disciples had gone into the town to buy food.)

⁹The Samaritan woman said to him, "You are a Jew and I am a Samaritan woman. How can you ask me for a drink?" (For Jews do not associate with Samaritans.)

¹⁰Jesus answered her, "If you knew the gift of God and who it is that asks you for a drink, you would have asked him and he would have given you living water."

¹¹"Sir," the woman said, "you have nothing to draw with and the well is deep. Where can you get this living water? ¹²Are you greater than our father Jacob, who gave us the well and drank from it himself, as did also his sons and his flocks and herds?"

¹³Jesus answered, "Everyone who drinks this water will be thirsty again, ¹⁴but whoever drinks the water I give him will never thirst. Indeed,

the water I give him will become in him a spring of water welling up to eternal life."

[15]The woman said to him, "Sir, give me this water so that I won't get thirsty and have to keep coming here to draw water."

[16]He told her, "Go, call your husband and come back."

[17]"I have no husband," she replied.

Jesus said to her, "You are right when you say you have no husband. [18]The fact is, you have had five husbands, and the man you now have is not your husband. What you have just said is quite true."

[19]"Sir," the woman said, "I can see that you are a prophet. [20]Our fathers worshiped on this mountain, but you Jews claim that the place where we must worship is in Jerusalem."

[21]Jesus declared, "Believe me, woman, a time is coming when you will worship the Father neither on this mountain nor in Jerusalem. [22]You Samaritans worship what you do not know; we worship what we do know, for salvation is from the Jews. [23]Yet a time is coming and has now come when the true worshipers will worship the Father in spirit and truth, for they are the kind of worshipers the Father seeks. [24]God is spirit, and his worshipers must worship in spirit and in truth."

[25]The woman said, "I know that Messiah" (called Christ) "is coming. When he comes, he will explain everything to us."

[26]Then Jesus declared, "I who speak to you am he."

[27]Just then his disciples returned and were surprised to find him talking with a woman. But no one asked, "What do you want?" or "Why are you talking with her?"

[28]Then, leaving her water jar, the woman went back to the town and said to the people, [29]"Come, see a man who told me everything I ever did. Could this be the Christ?" [30]They came out of the town and made their way toward him.

. . . .

[39]Many of the Samaritans from that town believed in him because of the woman's testimony, "He told me everything I ever did." [40]So when the Samaritans came to him, they urged him to stay with them, and he stayed two days. [41]And because of his words many more became believers.

[42]They said to the woman, "We no longer believe just because of what you said; now we have heard for ourselves, and we know that this man really is the Savior of the world."

Consider Where You Fit in This Story

Weary from a long journey, Jesus engaged a Samaritan woman in a conversation that not only changed her life, but also her whole village. The Samaritan woman stands in stark contrast to Nicodemus. Remember that Nicodemus was male, of the Jewish social elite, orthodox in faith, a religious teacher, who was assumed to be highly moral. Too, he had a name. This person, on the other hand, was a woman, a Samaritan, rejected socially, unorthodox in faith, with no status in the Samaritan religion, with blatantly immoral behavior. She was Sychar's five times (and counting) desperate housewife. Too, her name is not even given.

Here is the danger for us: that we become so consumed with our consumerism that we are no longer consumed with God's mission in the world.

When we read a story, we typically identify with some character in the narrative. Their struggles and victories become ours. What about this story? Do you identify with the disciples? with the woman? with the neighbors? Who are you in this story? The role of Savior is already taken, but what about the others?

Do you find the disciples inspiring, or tiring? Have you ever felt like this woman—going about your ordinary tasks, with all of your own problems, and then out of nowhere God enters your world? Or are you like the neighbors, who hear that God is up to something and have to go and see for themselves?

After Jesus, our ultimate hero, the heroine of this story is the woman who was a five-time divorcee and was living with yet another man. How did she become a heroine? Her connection with Christ transformed her, liberating her to a new purpose for life, that of sharing God's love with others. Never mind that Jesus' disciples had been right there among her fellow townspeople and apparently not said a word about Jesus coming to town. The disciples' first concern was getting something to eat. Jesus' first concern was planting and reaping a great harvest of souls.

We must ask again what it means to be a church sent into the world.

Here is the danger for us: that we become so consumed with our consumerism that we are no longer consumed with God's mission in the world. Until we hunger for God and to do the work of God more than we hunger for food, clothes, and possessions, we will be ineffective in our

Growing in Discipleship

The Samaritan woman grew spiritually as she grew in her awareness of Jesus' identity. In John 4:9, Jesus was only a Jewish male to her. But in 4:19, she saw him as "a prophet." Prophets in the Old Testament were spokespeople for God. They specialized more in proclaiming God's message than in predicting the future.

Later, in 4:29, she told the people in her town what had happened. She asked, "Could this be the Christ?" The promised Messiah was often envisioned as a ruling king who would restore the political fortunes of Israel. But in the Samaritan woman's view, he would be a teacher who would proclaim all things to all peoples.

---

mission to the world. Let us make connections with God and with others that lead to transformation and to mission. We must ask again what it means to be a church sent into the world.

Abandoning the Urgent to Accomplish the Important (4:1–4)

To share in the work of God's harvest, we must intentionally schedule our time to connect with the individuals who need the Lord the most. In John 4:1–3, we discover that Jesus and his disciples were enjoying a successful ministry in Judea. But the Pharisees heard, and Jesus left, avoiding a confrontation that might lead to his death before the appointed time.

> . . . We must intentionally schedule our time to connect with the individuals who need the Lord the most.

Many of the disciples would have been excited to return to their home area of Galilee. They were headed home to their families, home to their familiar places. Along the way, John 4:4 tells us that Jesus "had to go" through Samaria. The phrase conveys moral necessity. Why? There were other well-traveled routes for making the trip. Jesus "had to go through Samaria" because he had an appointment to keep that would affect not only this woman but the spiritual destiny of this city. He left a revival in Judea to speak to a five-time divorcee in Samaria.

Have we consecrated our calendars to Christ? If our eyes are open, we will see people as Jesus did and keep the divine appointments Jesus sets for us each day. Just as the disciples left Jesus to go and get food, often the temporal needs of our lives crowd out the greater spiritual needs of people in our world. We do not have to eat, as Jesus later said to the disciples, but we do have to bring in the harvest.

Abdicating Cultural Rules in Favor of Spiritual Relationships (4:5–9)

Jesus' vulnerability and transparency led to an unlikely conversation that surprised his disciples. In John 1, we learned that "The Word became flesh" (John 1:14). This story in John 4 shows us that Jesus was fully human. He experienced both exhaustion and thirst in 4:6–7, and presumed hunger in 4:31. He asked the woman for water, and she was surprised, according to 4:9.

Like Jesus, we must distinguish between cultural and spiritual rules and avoid the trap of condemning others for cultural reasons. When we read 4:7–9 we read them as simple statements of fact. When first-century Jews learned what Jesus did in verse 7, though, they would have gasped. This was scandalous: a Jewish man talked with a Samaritan woman. It would have made the local news—and it did, which is precisely what Jesus intended!

Have we consecrated our calendars to Christ?

Jesus broke two cultural rules here. First, as a man, he should not have spoken to a woman. She herself recognized this in her question in 4:9. Culturally, this conversation was a taboo. Religious rules of the day said men should not speak with women in public, even if they were husband and wife.

But Jesus spoke with this woman, surprising even his disciples (4:27). For Jesus, the value of helping this woman transcended the importance of keeping cultural mores.

We see the second cultural rule Jesus broke in 4:9, too. We see the woman questioning Jesus' behavior as a Jew asking a Samaritan for water. The Jews did not "associate" with the Samaritans. If Jesus had kept this rule, then she would have been lost. But Jesus flouted the rules that everybody knew he was supposed to keep. Why? Because love trumps legalism. Because relationship supersedes cultural rules.

Who are our Samaritans? Who are those with whom we will not speak? Why not?

Jesus did not wink at the sin of broken relationships in her life, but he did not cut her off from relationship with himself. Like Jesus, we must manifest God's love in our lives. The real cost of a church fulfilling its potential is not primarily financial but relational. Are we willing to pay the price of building bridges of relationship to the people who need Christ the most?

Quenching Spiritual Thirst (4:10–30)

Jesus answered the woman's objection by offering living water if she would only ask for it (4:10). In that arid region of the world, wells are necessary because no perpetual streams exist in the area. Jesus' promise of living water sounded to her like a rushing river generated by perpetual springs. Unaware of such a source, she pushed back, recognizing his obvious inability to draw water from Jacob's famous well there. Her reference to Jacob offered common ground for her as a Samaritan with Jesus. The Samaritans, like the Jews, also descended from Jacob. In truth, Jesus offered a spiritual water that quenches the thirst of a person's soul. She misunderstood but wanted the water so that she would not have to come and draw water from the well.

Like Jesus, we must distinguish between cultural and spiritual rules and avoid the trap of condemning others for cultural reasons.

Relentlessly, Jesus led her to the revelation of the secret she had been keeping and that had been keeping her (4:16). When Jesus invited her to go and get her husband, she denied that she had a husband. We see Jesus' divinity, when, looking into her soul, Jesus revealed that he knew she had been married many times and was now living with a man who was not her husband. Spiritually, her serial relationships revealed the thirst for something more than this world has to offer. In this passage, Jesus did two things. First he told her who *he* was, and then he showed her who *she* was.

Once the woman realized that Jesus knew about her love life, she opted to switch to a safer subject, a historical subject, the right place to worship God (4:19–20). Jesus turned the historical debate of the proper place to

41

Worshiping in Truth

In our lifetime, truth has been challenged. Regularly we read of leaders in various fields who willingly deceive others. If we wish to represent authentically the One who is truth, we must live the truth and tell the truth. Carefully consider: How do you need to fulfill Ephesians 4:14–15 by speaking the truth in love?

worship into a moment of deep insight into the character of God. In what might have been a "worship war," Jesus moved beyond the importance of Mount Gerizim (in Samaria) versus Mount Zion (Jerusalem) as the locus of worship. He emphasized that authentic worshipers must worship God in Spirit and in truth (4:23).

Since God is Spirit, God is present everywhere. Growing up in a military family, I moved many times, and I lived most of my childhood years in Germany. I discovered as a boy that our God is not limited to a location. To worship in Spirit is to know the God who comes to us, counsels us, and convicts us (14:15–17, 26; 16:8).

To worship in truth is to tell the truth (4:18) and to base our worship in authentic relationship with the Father who seeks us. God has come to us like a Father seeking a prodigal. In fact, Jesus said that more than we ever seek God, God is seeking us as worshipers who will worship in truth. Truth is not just a principle as Pilate suggested in John 18:38. In John 14:6, Jesus personalized truth when he said, "I am the way and the truth and the life."

. . . Love trumps legalism.

Telling Our Story So That Others May Believe (4:39–42)

As the woman headed into the village to report on her conversation with Jesus and her conviction about who he was (4:28–30), Jesus' disciples encouraged him to eat. Then Jesus reminded them that life is about more than food. He called on them to open their "eyes and look at the fields! They are ripe for harvest" (4:35).

Once the woman placed her trust in Jesus and became convinced that he was the Messiah, she determined to tell others. Her testimony brought the spiritual harvest of the village. In the end, the Samaritans drew a wonderful conclusion about Jesus. They no longer saw Jesus as just another Jew. Too, Jesus was more than a prophet and even more than a teaching Messiah. The crowds came to believe that Jesus is "the Savior of the world" (4:42). A man who spoke to a Samaritan woman and stayed in her town for two days could not be the Savior of Jews alone. The Samaritan villagers' words reflect the insight of John 3:17: "For God did not send his Son into the world to condemn the world, but to save the world through him." Jesus is the Savior of the Jews, the Samaritans, and all in the world who will believe in him.

> *Jesus is the Savior of the Jews, the Samaritans, and all in the world who will believe in him.*

Often new believers are effective evangelists because they have a larger network of friends who are pre-Christians. Sometimes our work for Christ within the church insulates and isolates us from the people who need our message the most.

When we tell the story of what Christ has done for us, two great opportunities emerge. First, people may believe in Christ because of our stories. Second, they may believe in Christ because through our stories we introduce them to God's greater story and God's story becomes their story. In this way, they personalize the message and take it to heart. Somebody has defined evangelism as *one hungry beggar telling another hungry beggar where to find bread.*[1] Maybe we can tell them about the Source of living water, too!

QUESTIONS

1. Jesus left an active ministry in Judea to go through Samaria. Is God calling us to leave some urgent work for something more important?

2. In what ways can you make time to get to know pre-Christian neighbors or co-workers?

3. How did Jesus' humanity facilitate the dialogue with the woman in John 4:6–7? Are you willing to be vulnerable and transparent in order to reach others with the gospel?

4. Jews did not dialogue with Samaritans. Who are your "Samaritans"? Is there a group of people whom you do not like based on their background, beliefs, or behavior? How can you build a bridge to that group of people?

5. The confession of this woman to her townspeople was, "Come, see a man who told me everything I ever did" (John 4:29). What is your story? How have you encountered Christ in an unmistakable way that you can tell to everyone around you?

NOTES

1. D.T. Niles from Ceylon. See *20 Centuries of Great Preaching: An Encyclopedia of Preaching*, Clyde M. Fant, Jr., and William M. Pinson, Jr., eds. (Waco, Texas: Word Books Publisher, 1971), XII:174.

Focal Text
John 5:1–24

Background
John 5

Main Idea
Jesus' claim on our lives transcends all human rules and agendas.

Question to Explore
In what ways do we need to "honor the Son"?

Study Aim
To identify specific ways in which we need to "honor the Son"

Study and Action Emphases

- Affirm the Bible as our authoritative guide for life and ministry
- Share the gospel with all people
- Develop a growing, vibrant faith
- Obey and serve Jesus by meeting physical, spiritual, and emotional needs
- Equip people for servant leadership

LESSON FOUR

Honoring the Son

Quick Read
Jesus made a man physically well and invited him to choose whether he would be spiritually whole as well. Because Jesus healed him on the Sabbath, Jesus' opponents persecuted him.

What do we really want from God? I love the story of the mother and son who were outside when a tornado surprised them. The mother clung to a tree and tried to hold her son, but the swirling winds carried him into the sky. He was gone. The woman began to weep and pray: "Please, O Lord, bring back my boy! He's all I have. I'd do anything not to lose him. If you'll bring him back, I'll serve you all of my days."

Suddenly the boy toppled from the sky, right at her feet. He was a bit mussed up, but safe and sound. His mother joyfully brushed him off. Then she stopped, looked to the sky, and said, "He had a hat, Lord."

Sometimes when God offers us what we ask, we are not content, and we ungratefully ask for more. Others have the opposite problem. Sometimes we fail in our prayers, not by asking too much but by asking too little. What if we are too easily satisfied? When Jesus asked a lame man whether he wanted to be made whole, the man was content to be healed physically, without ever receiving the power to become spiritually whole.

John 5:1–24

[1]Some time later, Jesus went up to Jerusalem for a feast of the Jews. [2]Now there is in Jerusalem near the Sheep Gate a pool, which in Aramaic is called Bethesda and which is surrounded by five covered colonnades. [3]Here a great number of disabled people used to lie—the blind, the lame, the paralyzed. [5]One who was there had been an invalid for thirty-eight years. [6]When Jesus saw him lying there and learned that he had been in this condition for a long time, he asked him, "Do you want to get well?"

[7]"Sir," the invalid replied, "I have no one to help me into the pool when the water is stirred. While I am trying to get in, someone else goes down ahead of me."

[8]Then Jesus said to him, "Get up! Pick up your mat and walk." [9]At once the man was cured; he picked up his mat and walked.

The day on which this took place was a Sabbath, [10]and so the Jews said to the man who had been healed, "It is the Sabbath; the law forbids you to carry your mat."

[11]But he replied, "The man who made me well said to me, 'Pick up your mat and walk.'"

[12]So they asked him, "Who is this fellow who told you to pick it up and walk?"

[13]The man who was healed had no idea who it was, for Jesus had slipped away into the crowd that was there.

14Later Jesus found him at the temple and said to him, "See, you are well again. Stop sinning or something worse may happen to you." **15**The man went away and told the Jews that it was Jesus who had made him well.

16So, because Jesus was doing these things on the Sabbath, the Jews persecuted him. **17**Jesus said to them, "My Father is always at his work to this very day, and I, too, am working." **18**For this reason the Jews tried all the harder to kill him; not only was he breaking the Sabbath, but he was even calling God his own Father, making himself equal with God.

19Jesus gave them this answer: "I tell you the truth, the Son can do nothing by himself; he can do only what he sees his Father doing, because whatever the Father does the Son also does. **20**For the Father loves the Son and shows him all he does. Yes, to your amazement he will show him even greater things than these. **21**For just as the Father raises the dead and gives them life, even so the Son gives life to whom he is pleased to give it. **22**Moreover, the Father judges no one, but has entrusted all judgment to the Son, **23**that all may honor the Son just as they honor the Father. He who does not honor the Son does not honor the Father, who sent him.

24"I tell you the truth, whoever hears my word and believes him who sent me has eternal life and will not be condemned; he has crossed over from death to life.

What Do We Want from God? (5:1–9)

Once again we see Jesus' concern for individual people. After Jesus kept his appointment with the woman at the well and healed an official's son in Galilee (John 4), he made his way back to Jerusalem. This was the place where the sick and hurting people were. They were lying there, waiting for the water to stir so they could climb in. The popular Jewish belief was that an angel stirred the water. So they waited there, hoping for healing. "Bethesda" means *the house of mercy*. The name found fulfillment when Jesus came there.

In this crowd of sick people, one stood out to Jesus. For thirty-eight years this man had been lying there, holding out hope. Every day for 13,870 days he must have hoped, *Maybe this will be the day.* Nearly four decades, over a third of a century, thinking every day, *If I could just walk.* What a long time to be lame!

Jesus asked the man: "Do you want to get well?" Perhaps the lame man thought, *Obviously, I want to get well, but I can't get into the pool. Don't mock me.* But Jesus was not mocking him.

47

The word for "want" in the question is the word *thelo*, which means *to will*. Do you *will* to get well? Jesus was not being facetious, and neither did Jesus ask the man to will himself to health. Jesus wanted to give him everything he wanted—and more. We might think, *Of course he wanted to be well. He wanted nothing more than to be well. All he wanted was to be well.* "Do you want to get well?" Doesn't the question seem absurd? Remember the question that formed the title of the popular television show, *Who Wants to Be a Millionaire?* Our first thought is, *Everybody!* So, of course the man wanted to be made whole! If we had been lying lame for thirty-eight years, we would want to be well, too, wouldn't we?

> Sometimes when God offers us what we ask, we are not content, and we ungratefully ask for more.

But Jesus saw beneath the surface. When this man began to explain why it wasn't his fault because nobody would help him, Jesus took away his excuse for not walking. Then the man had the responsibility to get up and walk on his own. When the man obeyed Jesus, the Pharisees condemned the man for carrying his mat on the Sabbath, thereby breaking their cultural interpretation of God's laws. Instead of taking responsibility, this formerly lame man said, *It's not my fault!* (See 5:11.) Later, when Jesus confronted him about the need to walk with God and avoid sin, the man turned Jesus in to the authorities (5:15).

This man settled for the good when he could have had the best. He found physical healing, but he missed the best of what Jesus had for him!

Jesus still has time for the individual. If we are hurting or afraid, Jesus cares about us. God wants to do more for us than we can imagine. We must never rule out the possibility that God wants to heal. This man didn't think that was possible, but it was God's design and purpose to heal him. Do we sometimes ask God to heal, without believing that God will?

God wants, though, to make us whole in every area of our lives—physical, emotional, and spiritual. Do we really want to be whole? We may say, *Well, if I could have my health, or if God would solve my financial burden, I would be satisfied.* Jesus, though, wants to make us truly whole. It is possible to be physically well and still not be whole. Only when we want to be whole, and when we want to have the integrity to walk with God, can we ever experience God's complete healing in our lives.

> What do we really want from God?

We who have received grace and goodness from God must now decide what we will do with the gift of life God has given us. It is possible to be blessed by God with enormous benefits in this life and never to be saved. Each of us must decide whether we want to be made whole.

What do we really want from God? To us, Jesus' question borders on the absurd, unless we read the rest of the story and realize Jesus was asking, *Is that all you want from me?* God has the power to heal us. Are we satisfied with only physical healing or maybe financial help? Is that *all* we want, or do we want to *know God?* Do we want to be whole? Jesus is the only one who can make us physically well, but Jesus also wants to make us spiritually well!

What Will We Do for God? (5:9–15)

Each of us must decide what we will do when we encounter Christ. Notice that the man obeyed Jesus. However, when the Jewish leaders confronted him, he would not take responsibility for his actions. Not only was it somebody else's fault that he could not get in the water (John 5:7), but in 5:11 he acted as though it was Jesus' fault that he was carrying his mat. When Jesus came back to him, Jesus, his Healer, said to him in effect, *You received all that you wanted from me. You are well physically.*

The Jews

Along with the simple story of Jesus' healing of the lame man, we discover that Jesus' opponents were at work behind the scenes. They were the first to notice that the healed man was carrying his mat on the Sabbath. This issue reemerges in the narrative in John 5:16. The Jews persecuted Jesus in 5:16, eliciting a response from Jesus in 5:17. Also in 5:17, they sought to kill him for calling God his Father and for breaking the Sabbath.

This collective title, "the Jews," does not describe all Jews of that particular time, much less Jews living today. Within the story of John, the term "Jews" often refers to those who opposed Jesus. Unfortunately, some have characterized John as anti-Semitic because of the abuses of Christians against Jews in history. In fact, Jesus and the formerly lame man were also Jews. The Jews in this instance were culpable, not because of their ethnic or religious identity, but because of their behavior. Any use of the Gospel of John as an excuse for hatred toward Jewish people represents an abuse of the Scriptures.

Jesus used the word "well" instead of *saved* in 5:14. But John 3:17 says Jesus came "to save," not just to heal. Later, Jesus expressed his desire that people be saved (5:34; 10:9;12:47). Sadly, Jesus did not say to him, *You have been saved.* Instead, Jesus said, "You are well again." Then Jesus urged him to stop sinning. We cannot assume that sin necessarily caused his lameness physically, but sin did cause his far more serious spiritual disability. After his healing, he walked, but he still did not walk with God.

> Sometimes we fail in our prayers, not by asking too much but by asking too little.

Remember in Mark 2:1–12, when Jesus healed another lame man, that Jesus forgave his sins and the man was converted. Not so this lame man. In his mind he was forever a victim, not taking responsibility for his life. When Jesus admonished him to "stop sinning" (John 5:14), he was saying, *You are physically well. But you will never be spiritually well until you step up and take responsibility for your own choices!* We have no evidence that this lame man ever accepted Christ as Savior. He accepted him only as healer.

By contrast, consider that in John 9:24–33 a man formerly blind also encountered these same critics, but he refused to join in the condemnation of Jesus. As Jesus' disciple and defender, he praised Jesus as the example of all that is good. He sacrificed his synagogue status for the sake of his Savior. He chose to be a victor instead of a victim.

> Each of us must decide what we will do when we encounter Christ.

Spiritual wholeness transcends physical wholeness. Entering a relationship with Christ includes taking responsibility for our own behavior and choices. With great privilege comes great responsibility.

When the Pharisees confronted the man for carrying his mat, the man seemed to mirror the mantra of recent years, *It's not my fault!* One cannot always assume someone has integrity. Not everybody wants to get well. Some people want to live their lives as victims so that they can wallow in their own misery.

What Does God Want from Us and for Us? (5:16–24)

Another story parallels the healing of the lame man. Behind the scenes, Jesus' opponents, characterized as "the Jews" (see article, "The Jews"), plotted against him and persecuted him for healing the man on the Sabbath. They expressed a greater concern for cultural rules than for spiritual relationship. They believed it was better to keep the customs than to heal a man lame for thirty-eight years. Jesus contended that the work of healing the man was in keeping with the continuing work of God in the world. The Word who created all things continued his creative work (1:3).

To this day, people who love the Scriptures battle with the issue of legalism. As a nineteen-year-old pastor of a rural church, I noticed a member of my congregation struggling with this one Sunday afternoon. I had gone to his home for a pleasant lunch with his family. Afterward, he looked out the window and sighed as he explained to me, "All of the cattle are in the pen. If I shut the gate now, I would save myself a lot of work. But I don't want to work on the Sabbath." I encouraged him to shut the gate.

They expressed a greater concern for cultural rules than for spiritual relationship.

True, we frequently miss the benefit of rest by failing to observe the Sabbath. But the point of the Sabbath is not to keep us from doing anything. Instead, we are to make the Sabbath a day of holy rest, reflection, and re-creation. This does not prohibit us from closing a gate or helping people. The work of the Father goes on twenty-four hours a day throughout the year. Jesus said to his disciples again in John 9:4, "As long as it is day, we must do the work of him who sent me."

Jesus once again flouted the Jewish leaders' legalistic interpretation of the Scriptures. In response to those who accused him of working on the Sabbath, Jesus answered that he worked even as his Father worked on the Sabbath. When they took offense at him for calling God his Father, he promptly used that expression over and over again in 5:19–24. Jesus defended his behavior as being consistent with that of the Father. Because the Father loves the Son, the Father shows him his work and uses him to give life to others. The Father entrusts all judgment to the Son so that all

The Focus of Ministry

Since the beginning of the church, there has been controversy about our priorities in continuing the ministry of Jesus in the world. Do we focus on meeting physical needs or spiritual needs? Do we serve only living bread, or the whole wheat variety as well? Read and consider Acts 6:1–7 as a case study of how the Holy Spirit guided the early church on this issue.

may honor the Son as they honor the Father. Jesus concluded by teaching that all who hear and believe have eternal life, escaping condemnation by passing from death to life.

Jesus effectively turned the tables on the legalists, showing them that they were not his judges but he was theirs.

In our response to Jesus, we choose either life or death. Which will we choose?

QUESTIONS

1. Why did Jesus ask the man whether he wanted to become well (5:6)?

2. In what ways did the man fail to take responsibility for his life (see 5:7, 11)? Are you in any way failing to take responsibility for your own life? Will you change that behavior? When?

3. How have Christians been unkind to Jews historically? Are you ever guilty of stereotyping others and marginalizing them? How will you address that behavior in your own life?

4. How are Christians guilty of pharisaical legalism in our day?

5. Are you regularly taking time for rest, reflection, and re-creation?

Focal Text

John 6:1–15, 25–35, 48–51, 66–69

Background

John 6

Main Idea

Jesus' provision for people's immediate needs signifies that he can supply their greatest need, spiritual life that comes through relationship with him.

Question to Explore

To whom besides Jesus can we go?

Study Aim

To decide to put priority on Jesus' supplying my spiritual needs rather than on the satisfaction of physical and material needs

Study and Action Emphases

- Affirm the Bible as our authoritative guide for life and ministry
- Share the gospel with all people
- Develop a growing, vibrant faith
- Obey and serve Jesus by meeting physical, spiritual, and emotional needs

LESSON FIVE

Relying On Our Only Hope

Quick Read

When the people sought to make Jesus an economic and political savior, he chose instead to give up his life to meet their greater spiritual needs.

Have you noticed the way we identify memories in connection with food? In my middle school years, my family, a military family, moved back to Germany. Opportunities for eating abounded. There was a grocery store behind us and an inn below us to the right, serving bratwurst and sauerkraut. In front of the inn stood an Italian ice cream stand that sold my favorite flavor—apricot. Still, none of these compared to the bakery that operated conveniently right beneath my room. For our two years there, every morning the smell of the fresh bread wafted its way upward to our apartment through our open windows and into my nostrils.

Some time during those years, I first read Jesus' words in Matthew 4:4 that said, "Man does not live on bread alone." Even so, I was glad the bakery was there.

Much of our human existence is caught up in the desire to find food. When Jesus fed the crowds bread and fish, they decided they liked the arrangement.

John 6:1–15, 25–35, 48–51, 66–69

[1]Some time after this, Jesus crossed to the far shore of the Sea of Galilee (that is, the Sea of Tiberias), [2]and a great crowd of people followed him because they saw the miraculous signs he had performed on the sick. [3]Then Jesus went up on a mountainside and sat down with his disciples. [4]The Jewish Passover Feast was near.

[5]When Jesus looked up and saw a great crowd coming toward him, he said to Philip, "Where shall we buy bread for these people to eat?" [6]He asked this only to test him, for he already had in mind what he was going to do.

[7]Philip answered him, "Eight months' wages would not buy enough bread for each one to have a bite!"

[8]Another of his disciples, Andrew, Simon Peter's brother, spoke up, [9]"Here is a boy with five small barley loaves and two small fish, but how far will they go among so many?"

[10]Jesus said, "Have the people sit down." There was plenty of grass in that place, and the men sat down, about five thousand of them. [11]Jesus then took the loaves, gave thanks, and distributed to those who were seated as much as they wanted. He did the same with the fish.

[12]When they had all had enough to eat, he said to his disciples, "Gather the pieces that are left over. Let nothing be wasted." [13]So they gathered them and filled twelve baskets with the pieces of the five barley loaves left over by those who had eaten.

14After the people saw the miraculous sign that Jesus did, they began to say, "Surely this is the Prophet who is to come into the world." **15**Jesus, knowing that they intended to come and make him king by force, withdrew again to a mountain by himself.

· ·

25When they found him on the other side of the lake, they asked him, "Rabbi, when did you get here?"

26Jesus answered, "I tell you the truth, you are looking for me, not because you saw miraculous signs but because you ate the loaves and had your fill. **27**Do not work for food that spoils, but for food that endures to eternal life, which the Son of Man will give you. On him God the Father has placed his seal of approval."

28Then they asked him, "What must we do to do the works God requires?"

29Jesus answered, "The work of God is this: to believe in the one he has sent."

30So they asked him, "What miraculous sign then will you give that we may see it and believe you? What will you do? **31**Our forefathers ate the manna in the desert; as it is written: 'He gave them bread from heaven to eat.'"

32Jesus said to them, "I tell you the truth, it is not Moses who has given you the bread from heaven, but it is my Father who gives you the true bread from heaven. **33**For the bread of God is he who comes down from heaven and gives life to the world."

34"Sir," they said, "from now on give us this bread."

35Then Jesus declared, "I am the bread of life. He who comes to me will never go hungry, and he who believes in me will never be thirsty.

· ·

48I am the bread of life. **49**Your forefathers ate the manna in the desert, yet they died. **50**But here is the bread that comes down from heaven, which a man may eat and not die. **51**I am the living bread that came down from heaven. If anyone eats of this bread, he will live forever. This bread is my flesh, which I will give for the life of the world."

· ·

66From this time many of his disciples turned back and no longer followed him.

67"You do not want to leave too, do you?" Jesus asked the Twelve.

68Simon Peter answered him, "Lord, to whom shall we go? You have the words of eternal life. **69**We believe and know that you are the Holy One of God."

Jesus Provides Food for the Multitude (6:1–15)

The multitudes were a welcome interruption for Jesus. Having withdrawn from the conflict of Jerusalem (John 5), Jesus sat down with his disciples in the posture of a teacher. Class had already begun, and he was preparing for a great small group time. The lesson was

. . . Jesus never saw people as a nuisance.

ready, and the disciples were all in their places with bright shining faces. But out of nowhere came the mob—that great mobile mass of humanity who came like locusts to devour the time and energy of the Lord. The disciples might have wondered, *Can't a Messiah carry on a ministry around here?* Sometimes his disciples tried to push the people away. But Jesus never saw people as a nuisance. So he asked in John 6:5, "Where shall we buy bread for these people to eat?"

We have not come far enough in our discipleship if we still see people as a nuisance. Even a cursory glance reveals that we live in a world with a great crowd of people who shoulder enormous needs. What will we do about those needs? Philip was skeptical about the cost of feeding the crowd. Meanwhile, Andrew, the disciple who was always bringing somebody to Jesus (1:41–42; 12:20–22), brought a boy with five small barley loaves and two small fish.

The Lord's Supper

To this day, when we partake of the Lord's Supper, we affirm our faith in Jesus' unique sacrifice for our sins. Believing in Jesus still brings eternal life.

Different denominations have interpreted the Lord's Supper in various ways. Some believe in *transubstantiation*, the physical transformation of the bread into Jesus' body and the wine into his blood during the Lord's Supper. Others believe in *consubstantiation*, meaning that Christ is really present in the bread, but it is not his actual body. Baptists have not traditionally understood the bread to be literally Jesus' body. We do believe that Christ is present among his people as we remember his death in the Lord's Supper. We must be careful about calling the Lord's Supper "just a memorial," because this minimizes the importance of the Supper.

Ponder in John 6:11 Jesus' expression of gratitude for the bread before he broke it. The Greek word for thanksgiving gives us the word *Eucharist*, a common name for the Lord's Supper. When we realize that Jesus knew the bread represented his body, how do we account for his gratitude in breaking it? Are we grateful, truly grateful, for his gift? While many in our world drink to forget, we eat and drink to remember God's great gift to us.

While we are figuring out the plan, we need to know that our God is the God of the smallest details. John explained, referring to the question in 6:5, "He asked this only to test him, for he already had in mind what he was going to do" (6:6)! Jesus already knew what he would do. The great question is this: *Have we come to know the God who knows?*

All four Gospels tell this miracle story of the feeding of the 5,000 (see Matthew 14:13–21; Mark 6:30–44; Luke 9:10–17). Each evangelist tells us something unique about the experience. John's contribution is to give us a picture of a Jesus who was fully aware of his intentions when he invited his disciples to join him in caring for the multitude. Jesus knew. He knew the people were coming. He knew a boy had five loaves and two fish. He knew when he

Much of our human existence is caught up in the desire to find food.

fed the fish there would be baskets of fragments. He knew that after he fed them, the crowds who really did not know him would want him to be a king. Too, he knew that the disciples needed to know him better.

Some years ago I studied for a week at a seminary in Kentucky. At the head of the cafeteria line was a large pile of oranges. On a sign next to them, I saw these words: "Take only one orange—God is watching." I obeyed and then paused at the far end of the line. There I saw a large pile of chocolate chip cookies. Someone had written another sign: "Take all the cookies you want. God is back there watching the oranges."

We have not come far enough in our discipleship if we still see people as a nuisance.

God knows everything. But do we know him? The crowds wanted to believe that Jesus was the prophet predicted in Deuteronomy 18:18. They were looking for a political and economic savior, but Jesus knew they misunderstood his messiahship. So he withdrew from them. To this day, a misunderstanding of Jesus' messiahship leads to distorted discipleship. Many seek God only for the things he can give. Prominent pulpiteers promise health and prosperity. Can we say with Paul in Philippians 3:10, "I want to know Christ"? When we come to know the God who knows, we will come to care more for others than we do for our own needs. To know Jesus is to know that Jesus offers more than mere bread.

Jesus Promises Bread That Satisfies the Soul (6:25–35, 48–51)

Jesus offers more because after receiving only bread we hunger again. This crowd was no different. Sensing they had found a free meal ticket, they pursued Jesus again. After Jesus came to the disciples by walking on the water (John 6:16–21), they all arrived on the opposite shore of the Sea of Galilee.

> *. . . We live in a world with a great crowd of people who shoulder enormous needs.*

In John 6:25, the crowds found Jesus again. Jesus warned them about seeking him only for the temporary bread that feeds the body alone. Feigning spiritual interest, they wondered aloud about how to do the works of God. Jesus explained that the great work is believing in the One God has sent. In 6:31, they suggested that Jesus perform a sign like the miracle of manna, which they attributed to Moses. Jesus corrected them in 6:32: "It is not Moses who has given you the bread from heaven, but it is my Father who gives you the true bread from heaven."

While the crowds would easily have settled for more Mosaic manna, Jesus had come down from heaven as the true bread to give life to the world. Still, the crowds persisted in seeking a permanent supply of food (6:34), much as the woman at the well had asked for perpetual water (4:15). They made selfish demands because they had no interest in the great gift of God, which Jesus embodied. In 6:35, Jesus offered instead himself as the bread of life. Again in 6:48–51, Jesus explained that anyone who consumes his flesh, given for the life of the world, will live forever. In this way Jesus pointed to his crucifixion. Those who partake of Jesus'

"I Am"

The myriad books about Jesus in bookstores today reveal a strong thirst for knowledge about Jesus' identity. Only the Gospel of John reveals to us a wonderful spiritual dimension of Jesus' self-understanding through a series of "I am" sayings. In John 6:35, 48, Jesus proclaimed that he is "the bread of life" (see also 6:41, 51). Take time this week to review other "I am" sayings in the Gospel of John (8:12; 10:7, 9, 11, 14; 11:25; 14:6; 15:1, 5; see also 9:5). How do these self-disclosures of Jesus shape what we believe about Christ's identity?

crucified body by believing in Christ receive eternal life. Christ promised twice (6:40, 54) to raise these believers up "at the last day."

How often do we settle for less than God has in store for us? Our God invites us to find in him the satisfaction of all our desires. In Matthew 5:6, Jesus promised that those who "hunger and thirst for righteousness . . . will be filled." Do we thirst for God as did the psalmist in Psalms 42:1 and 63:1–5? God alone satisfies the desires of our souls.

> *To this day, a misunderstanding of Jesus' messiahship leads to distorted discipleship.*

A dear friend and campus minister at one of our Baptist colleges has endured many difficulties in her life. Whenever we ask her how she is, she answers with a single word: "Sustained." The grace of God given to us in Jesus sustains all of us. She is wise to know this truth.

Jesus Proclaims the Words of Life (6:66–69)

In John 6:52, "the Jews began to argue sharply" over Jesus' teachings. In John 6:61, even "his disciples were grumbling." John 6:66 tells us that some of his disciples simply left him that day because they found his teaching too hard to understand and live. But Jesus refused to soften the teaching to make it more palatable for their finicky spiritual taste. Instead, Jesus invited the ones who remained to decide whether they would also leave.

In this moment of decision, Simon Peter confessed his heart, "Lord, to whom shall we go? You have the words of eternal life" (6:68)! This great confession of Jesus as the "Holy One of God" (6:69) reminds us that Jesus' authentic followers were not following him for the free food and miracle show. Not by bread alone, but by the words of eternal life they found sustenance. They knew that Jesus alone was the answer for their lives.

> *They knew that Jesus alone was the answer for their lives.*

To this day, we can purchase bread in various venues, but we find the Bread of Life exclusively in Jesus Christ. When Peter called Jesus "the Holy One of God," he revealed deeper insight than the fickle crowds who merely wanted a messiah to feed their bodies. Jesus is not just the prophetic celebrity who will become a political king or economic savior. Jesus is the One who has been set apart as holy, sent by the Father.

QUESTIONS

1. What does the story of the feeding of the five thousand tell us about what Jesus knows (see John 6:6, 15)?

2. In chapter 6, different groups interacted with Jesus in different ways. What are the various groups? See if you can characterize the responses of each of these groups as positive or negative.

3. What did the crowds want when they mentioned the sign and the manna in John 6:30–31, 34?

4. How did "the Jews" respond to Jesus' invitation to partake of "the bread of life" in 6:41–42?

5. Why did Jesus say that they must eat his flesh and drink his blood (6:56)? What would be the result? What was the response in John 6:60?

6. Who left Jesus in verse 66? Why did they leave? Why did Jesus' true disciples stay, according to verses 68–69?

7. What part of this Scripture passage is most challenging to you to apply to yourself?

Focal Text

John 11:1–13,
17–27, 38–44

Background

John 11

Main Idea

Jesus provides eternal
life—including the
overcoming of physical
death—to everyone
who believes in him.

Question to Explore

Do you believe that
everyone who believes
in Jesus will never die?

Study Aim

To describe the difference that Jesus'
power as the resurrection and the life
makes when we believe in him

Study and Action Emphases

- Affirm the Bible as our authoritative guide for
  life and ministry
- Share the gospel with all people
- Develop a growing, vibrant faith

LESSON SIX

Believing in Jesus as the Resurrection and the Life

Quick Read

Because Jesus is the resurrection and the life, we
have nothing to fear.

The call came early on a Monday morning. An eighteen-year-old boy, recently ill with chicken pox, was experiencing a high fever and convulsions. I met the family at Hillcrest Baptist Medical Center in Waco and heard the devastating diagnosis: meningitis. Over the next several days, we kept prayerful vigil with the family in the intensive care waiting room, hoping for some sign of recovering life. None came. As a young pastor, just a few years older than this young man, I first came to grips with the harsh reality of sickness and suffering in our world.

On the road from Jericho to Jerusalem, just two miles from the holy city, was the village of Bethany. For a Savior who had no place to lay his head, Bethany became a respite where he lived and loved and laughed.

Doesn't it seem odd that when Jesus heard about the illness of Lazarus, instead of going to Lazarus immediately, Jesus waited, allowing his friend to die? Only then did Jesus go to Bethany, to Martha and Mary. How could Jesus be considered a compassionate Savior? He knew his friend was suffering and yet he waited.

Waiting was harder for Jesus than we can imagine, but Jesus was committed to doing the work of God within the will of God for the glory of God. So he waited. Our Lord was never bound by the tyranny of the urgent.

Some of us have asked God specifically for relief from some situation in our lives, and yet, instead of getting an answer, we perceive that the heavens are stone. We ask, and God waits. We learn from this story that no matter what happens, we must never forget that God loves us. In fact, because God loves us, God will let us go through pain sometimes but will ultimately lift us beyond the pain to a new and better understanding of his purpose for our lives. God can simultaneously love us and let us go through pain.

John 11:1–13, 17–27, 38–44

[1]Now a man named Lazarus was sick. He was from Bethany, the village of Mary and her sister Martha. [2]This Mary, whose brother Lazarus now lay sick, was the same one who poured perfume on the Lord and wiped his feet with her hair. [3]So the sisters sent word to Jesus, "Lord, the one you love is sick."

[4]When he heard this, Jesus said, "This sickness will not end in death. No, it is for God's glory so that God's Son may be glorified through it." [5]Jesus loved Martha and her sister and Lazarus. [6]Yet when he heard that Lazarus was sick, he stayed where he was two more days.

[7]Then he said to his disciples, "Let us go back to Judea."

[8] "But Rabbi," they said, "a short while ago the Jews tried to stone you, and yet you are going back there?"

[9] Jesus answered, "Are there not twelve hours of daylight? A man who walks by day will not stumble, for he sees by this world's light. [10] It is when he walks by night that he stumbles, for he has no light."

[11] After he had said this, he went on to tell them, "Our friend Lazarus has fallen asleep; but I am going there to wake him up."

[12] His disciples replied, "Lord, if he sleeps, he will get better." [13] Jesus had been speaking of his death, but his disciples thought he meant natural sleep.

. . . .

[17] On his arrival, Jesus found that Lazarus had already been in the tomb for four days. [18] Bethany was less than two miles from Jerusalem, [19] and many Jews had come to Martha and Mary to comfort them in the loss of their brother. [20] When Martha heard that Jesus was coming, she went out to meet him, but Mary stayed at home.

[21] "Lord," Martha said to Jesus, "if you had been here, my brother would not have died. [22] But I know that even now God will give you whatever you ask."

[23] Jesus said to her, "Your brother will rise again."

[24] Martha answered, "I know he will rise again in the resurrection at the last day."

[25] Jesus said to her, "I am the resurrection and the life. He who believes in me will live, even though he dies; [26] and whoever lives and believes in me will never die. Do you believe this?"

[27] "Yes, Lord," she told him, "I believe that you are the Christ, the Son of God, who was to come into the world."

. . . .

[38] Jesus, once more deeply moved, came to the tomb. It was a cave with a stone laid across the entrance. [39] "Take away the stone," he said.

"But, Lord," said Martha, the sister of the dead man, "by this time there is a bad odor, for he has been there four days."

[40] Then Jesus said, "Did I not tell you that if you believed, you would see the glory of God?"

[41] So they took away the stone. Then Jesus looked up and said, "Father, I thank you that you have heard me. [42] I knew that you always hear me, but I said this for the benefit of the people standing here, that they may believe that you sent me."

[43] When he had said this, Jesus called in a loud voice, "Lazarus, come out!" [44] The dead man came out, his hands and feet wrapped with strips of linen, and a cloth around his face.

When God Waits (11:1–13)

Jesus enjoyed a rich friendship with Lazarus and his two sisters, Mary and Martha. John identified Mary as the one who would pour oil on Jesus' feet and wipe them with her hair. She had been delivered from her sins. In Luke 10:38–42, Mary had listened as Jesus taught, and Martha had worried about the details of the food for the occasion. Jesus also had a history with Lazarus. Listen to the message of John 11:3: "Lord, the one you love is sick." Hear the implication: *Lord, this is not just anybody. This is the one you love as a treasured friend.*

> *Our Lord was never bound by the tyranny of the urgent.*

We must be clear: there was nothing wrong with the request of the sisters. First, it was true that Jesus was Lord. They knew Jesus' power. Second, it was true that Jesus loved Lazarus. In fact, John 11:5 tells us that Jesus not only loved these three with *philos* love—friendship love—as the sisters suggested in 11:3 but with *agape* love, the highest kind of love. Even the Jewish leaders acknowledged that Jesus loved Lazarus when they saw Jesus weep (John 11:36).

Ordinary human love would call on us to do all that we can in a situation like this. That is what makes Jesus' response so startling. "Yet when he heard that Lazarus was sick, he stayed where he was for two more days" (11:6). As we read these words, the meaning sounds like this: *Jesus loved Martha, Mary, and Lazarus with an unconditional love; therefore, when he heard about the sickness of Lazarus, he did nothing.* Because Jesus loved Lazarus, he waited? The crowd knew Jesus loved him, according to verse 36, but

> *We learn from this story that no matter what happens, we must never forget that God loves us.*

they wondered aloud, *If Jesus did love him, and Jesus had the power to open the eyes of the blind, couldn't Jesus have saved him* (11:37)? Here is the point: If Jesus had just loved Lazarus as a friend, he would have gone—but Jesus also loved him as a Savior.

Mystified, Jesus' disciples heard his response in 11:4: "This sickness will not end in death." In fact, Lazarus did die physically, but spiritually he was alive. Jesus waited for Lazarus's sake and for God's glory. Shedding further light, Jesus, who uniquely possessed the power to overcome death and give life, viewed Lazarus's death as sleep (11:11–12).

Our temptation in times of pain is to question either God's love or God's power. Both doubts are in error. Psalm 62:11–12 declares, "One thing God has spoken, two things have I heard: that you, O God, are strong, and that you, O Lord, are loving." God loves us and lets us go through pain. In fact, sometimes the pain that leads to God's greater work in your life is the proof of God's love. Paul certainly experienced this with his thorn in the flesh. In 2 Corinthians 12:7–10, we learn that God chose to give Paul his all-sufficient grace instead of removing his thorn.

Often in my life, I would have let God love me as a friend, when God wanted to love me as a Father. At times, I would have settled for so much less than God had for me both in relationships and in opportunities of service to the church. We must not settle for less than God has for us. Would we settle for happiness in the moment, when God purposes holiness for eternity? So, in answer to the question, *Where is God when I am hurting?* know that God is on his way. Even when God waits and we can't see him, God is always on his way.

The Arrival of Life (11:17–27)

By the time Jesus arrived, Lazarus had been dead for four days. Mary and Martha were well into their grieving process with the help of neighbors

---

Opposition to Jesus

Once Jesus healed Lazarus, the religious leaders of the day, characterized as "Jews" and as "chief priests and Pharisees," determined to kill Jesus (see John 11:45–53). They feared that Jesus' miraculous signs would continue to lead people to believe in him and that this political clout would raise the Romans' ire at Jesus' presumed kingship. Blinded by their envy and hatred, they plotted to kill the One who is the resurrection and the life. In their outrage, they also wanted to kill Lazarus (12:9–11). Ironically, Lazarus's story predicts the ultimate outcome of their efforts.

In 11:49–51, we see that Caiaphas, the high priest at the time, was willing to let "one man die for the people" instead of allowing "the whole nation to perish." Even Caiaphas did not realize the significance of his statement. Jesus would indeed die for the people and for all of "the scattered children of God" (11:52). The religious leaders thought they were saving the nation by killing Jesus, but Jesus voluntarily went to the cross to save the world.

---

from Jerusalem. Martha expressed her deep disappointment and held on to hope when she encountered Jesus. "Lord . . . if you had been here, my brother would not have died. But I know that even now God will give whatever you ask" (John 11:21–22). Martha had seen Jesus perform miracles before, and so she knew that he could have prevented Lazarus's death. Mary echoed this sentiment when she fell weeping at Jesus' feet with the same words in 11:32. But did they know that Jesus could bring Lazarus back to life? Jesus offered hope of resurrection to Martha in 11:23, but in 11:24 she deferred that hope to "the resurrection at the last day."

> *Our temptation in times of pain is to question either God's love or God's power.*

In one of the greatest pronouncements of his ministry, Jesus identified himself as the embodiment of the resurrection and the life (11:25). The corollary offers hope to all of us who live in the valley of the shadow of death: "He who believes in me will live even though he dies, and whoever lives and believes in me will never die" (11:25–26). Even Jesus' announcement is an invitation to faith. He asked (11:26), "Do you believe this?" We cannot miss Martha's profession of faith: "I believe that you are the Christ, the Son of God, who was to come into the world" (11:27). Like Peter in 6:68–69, and the blind man in 9:35–38, Martha recognized that Jesus is the Messiah, the Son of God. In this Gospel, only Thomas's confession in 20:28 exceeds hers. In the presence of the risen Lord, Thomas said, "My Lord and My God!"

Hope Revived (11:38–44)

Once again, we see Jesus' humanity as he wept in 11:35. Mary's tears moved him, and he asked to go to the grave. We see evidence of Jesus' concern in John 11:33, 35, and 38. Why was Jesus so greatly disturbed? Do we see Jesus responding to the stark and harsh reality of death? Or was Jesus troubled by the misunderstanding of the crowd, who questioned his decision to delay in coming to Lazarus? Jesus was marching steadily toward Jerusalem for the last time in his ministry. In 11:16, Thomas voiced the expectation of Jesus and the disciples when they made their way to Bethany: "Let us also go, that we may die with him." This story

> *We are not alone in our pain.*

is the turning point in John's Gospel and Jesus' ministry. Certainly all of these factors influenced Jesus' feelings at this point. Even more, though, we see in John's Gospel that Jesus was human. He experienced exhaustion, thirst, and hunger. Here we see the genuine concern and empathy Jesus felt for those who are suffering. We are not alone in our pain.

Martha's concern in 11:39 about the decomposition of her brother's body revealed her elementary understanding of Jesus' earlier pronouncement of his power over death. She still didn't understand who Jesus was. So Jesus tested her faith again in 11:40: "Did not I tell you that if you believed you would see the glory of God?" From the beginning of the story of Lazarus, Jesus knew that this sickness would result in God's glory and the glorification of God's Son through it. Jesus revealed his true identity in this climactic moment.

. . . Jesus was committed to doing the work of God within the will of God for the glory of God.

Listen carefully to Jesus' words. Calling God "Father," Jesus showed that he really believed he was God's Son, as Martha had said in 11:27. Calling Lazarus by name, Jesus had the audacity to believe that he had power over death. If nothing had happened, Jesus would have been revealed as a fraud and reviled for it. But imagine the dramatic moment when the people heard a stirring in the grave, and the dead man came out. Someone has suggested that Jesus called Lazarus specifically by name, because if he had not said, "Lazarus," every person in the cemetery would have risen! Such is the power of the One who is the resurrection and the life. Christianity has been "buried" many times by

Who Is Jesus?

In the Gospel of John, we find a number of confessions of faith moving upward through the narrative toward Thomas's exclamation, "My Lord and my God" (John 20:28). So from the exalted titles of Word, Light, and Lamb in John 1, we see progressive recognition of Jesus. He is more than a man, greater than John and Moses, and more than just a prophet. Jesus is the Son of God.

The formerly blind man in John 9 grew in discipleship as he opened his spiritual eyes in perception of Jesus' messiahship. When all had forsaken the formerly blind man, Jesus came to him and asked (9:35), "Do you believe in the Son of Man?" Ultimately, the man called Jesus "Lord" and believed (9:38). Thomas's doubt gave way to great faith when he called Jesus, "My Lord and My God" (20:28).

detractors only to rise again because we have a God who knows his way out of the grave.

Some years ago, a young woman entered Baptist St. Anthony's hospital in Amarillo, Texas, for a routine surgery. She emerged from the surgery fine but then started having headaches. Then, before long, the doctors discovered that an aneurysm had exploded at the base of her brain. She was placed on life support, and her family and church family began the prayer vigil of hope that she would awaken. It was not to happen. So the doctors told the family that she could be taken off life support. Her husband gave each of the family members time with her. Then he asked the pastor, Dr. Howie Batson of First Baptist Church, Amarillo, Texas, to wait outside the door while he said goodbye.

Because Jesus is the resurrection and the life, we have nothing to fear.

After about thirty minutes Howie saw the young husband get up, move around the room, and then walk out resolutely. Howie asked, "Have you said goodbye?" The young man said, "Yes, we're ready." Howie went in and discovered that he had opened his wife's Bible to John 3:16, rested it across her lap, and placed her hand pointing at that verse. The only way the young husband could walk out was with the knowledge that those who believe in Christ will never perish but have everlasting life. As the young woman's heart stopped beating, Howie quoted that verse, "For God so loved the world that he gave his one and only Son, that whoever believes in him shall not perish but have eternal life."

Do you believe this? Because Jesus is the resurrection and the life, we have nothing to fear.

QUESTIONS

1. Do you remember a time when you were waiting for God and you felt God was waiting too long? What was the outcome of that experience? Do you believe that God can simultaneously love us and let us suffer?

2. Martha and Mary fought for faith as they tried to trust Jesus. Can you see the progression in their faith in him? Is your faith ever a matter of two steps forward, one step back?

3. How does this story inform our ministry to those who are suffering the loss of a loved one? As comforters, is there ever a time simply to remain silent and minister by our presence alone?

4. What does this story tell us about Jesus' identity? How does that help us as we experience sickness and face death in our own lives and the lives of loved ones?

Jesus' Farewell Message to His Disciples

The hour had come. Jesus knew that his time on earth was coming to an end. He spent his final evening before the crucifixion alone with his disciples. A lifetime of teaching was wrapped up in a single evening. How could Jesus prepare them for a future that included persecution and even death? John 13—17 contains Jesus' farewell message to the disciples as he prepared them for his death on the cross the very next day.

The night started out as a celebration leading up to the Passover feast. The disciples must have been excited about spending time with Jesus away from the crowds. The atmosphere quickly changed when Jesus got up and began washing their feet. Could this be happening? Slaves were supposed to wash feet, and their Leader was performing the lowliest of duties!

An awkward silence filled the room as Jesus' penetrating look searched the hearts of each disciple. Jesus asked (John 13:12), "Do you know what I have done to you?"[1] Jesus exhorted them to follow his example in their service to one another.

The disciples continued to listen as Jesus talked about leaving them. Although Jesus' voice was determined and strong, the Twelve exchanged glances, and the feeling of impending doom overwhelmed them. Jesus reassured them that he would provide for them through the presence of the Holy Spirit after he was gone. Jesus reminded them of his relationship with the Father and promised to return for them after he had prepared a place for them.

Using the metaphor of a vine and branches, Jesus emphasized the necessity of total dependence on him for sustenance. The section closes with Jesus praying for the protection of the disciples. He prayed for future Christians and asked God to send them on mission throughout the world and to protect the unity of the church.

John 13, to be studied in lesson seven, focuses on Jesus' demonstration of the kind of love the disciples needed to show—the kind that washed one another's dirty feet. Lesson eight is on the peace that Jesus provides his followers and is on Scripture passages in John 14. Lesson nine, which is on Scriptures selected from John 15, focuses on the need to be productive as Christians, which we can do only by staying joined to Jesus. Lesson ten is a study of John 17, Jesus' prayer for his followers then and now.

UNIT TWO. JESUS' FAREWELL MESSAGE TO HIS DISCIPLES

Lesson 7	Practice Love Beyond the Limits	John 13:1–17, 34–35
Lesson 8	Rest Assured	John 14:1–11, 15–18, 25–27
Lesson 9	Stay United to Jesus	John 15:1–17
Lesson 10	What Jesus Wants for His Followers	John 17

NOTES

1. Unless otherwise indicated, all Scripture quotations in this introduction and lessons 7–10 are from the New American Standard Bible (1995 edition).

Focal Text

John 13:1–17, 34–35

Background

John 13

Main Idea

In following Jesus, we are to allow Jesus' love to so permeate our lives that we embody it in our relationships with others.

Question to Explore

To what extent and in what ways does Jesus' love motivate you to love others?

Study Aim

To decide on ways I will allow Jesus' love to so permeate my life that I embody it in my relationships with others

Study and Action Emphases

- Affirm the Bible as our authoritative guide for life and ministry
- Share the gospel with all people
- Develop a growing, vibrant faith
- Value all people as created in the image of God
- Obey and serve Jesus by meeting physical, spiritual, and emotional needs
- Equip people for servant leadership

LESSON SEVEN

Practice Love Beyond the Limits

Quick Read

Jesus washed the feet of his disciples as an expression of his deep love for them. Jesus expected his disciples to be willing to serve one another in the same manner.

73

When I was in high school, the Sunday School teachers at my church illustrated this lesson on John 13 in a creative way. As each of us entered the room, we were greeted by a teacher who directed us to sit down while another teacher polished our shoes. My reaction was just like Peter's when Jesus washed the feet of the disciples. I told them that it was not right, and I would not let any of them shine my shoes. They gave me some time to think, but they would not allow me into the room until I agreed to let them shine my shoes. My first inclination was to turn around and leave. I did not really have anywhere to go, but I was simply determined I would not let them polish my shoes! My parents had taught me respect for my elders, and I liked and respected my teachers.

As I was thinking in the hallway, it struck me that I was just like Peter. I did not understand true discipleship or the servant nature of the Christian life. My human concept of the way things should be did not include leaders becoming servants. My pride stood in the way of receiving this act of service from my teachers. When I went back into the room, it was with a totally new understanding of what Jesus did for his disciples on that evening before his death.

John gives a fairly lengthy account of what is known as the Last Supper. He is the only one of the Gospel writers who includes Jesus washing his disciples' feet, and yet the Gospel of John does not mention the Lord's Supper itself. John was probably writing for Christians who were familiar with some of the other writings, and the Lord's Supper already played a part in the worship of the early church. John included the account of Jesus washing the feet of his disciples because it underscores the servant nature of Jesus and emphasizes Jesus' admonishment to his disciples that they serve one another in the same manner.

Although some churches practice footwashing as an ordinance or sacrament, Baptists have not traditionally interpreted it in this manner. Baptists have interpreted the significance of footwashing to be in actual service to others, rather than the ritual washing of feet.

An Incredible Act of Love (13:1–5)

Jesus was keenly aware that his time on earth was coming to a close. Jesus came into the world, and now it was time to return to the Father. The world rejected the One who made it (John 1:10–11). So Jesus now turned to his closest friends during his final hours on earth. Verse 1 says he knew

John 13:1–17, 34–35

¹Now before the Feast of the Passover, Jesus knowing that His hour had come that He would depart out of this world to the Father, having loved His own who were in the world, He loved them to the end. ²During supper, the devil having already put into the heart of Judas Iscariot, the son of Simon, to betray Him, ³Jesus, knowing that the Father had given all things into His hands, and that He had come forth from God and was going back to God, ⁴got up from supper, and laid aside His garments; and taking a towel, He girded Himself.

⁵Then He poured water into the basin, and began to wash the disciples' feet and to wipe them with the towel with which He was girded. ⁶So He came to Simon Peter. He said to Him, "Lord, do You wash my feet?" ⁷Jesus answered and said to him, "What I do you do not realize now, but you will understand hereafter." ⁸Peter said to Him, "Never shall You wash my feet!" Jesus answered him, "If I do not wash you, you have no part with Me." ⁹Simon Peter said to Him, "Lord, then wash not only my feet, but also my hands and my head." ¹⁰Jesus said to him, "He who has bathed needs only to wash his feet, but is completely clean; and you are clean, but not all of you." ¹¹For He knew the one who was betraying Him; for this reason He said, "Not all of you are clean."

¹²So when He had washed their feet, and taken His garments and reclined at the table again, He said to them, "Do you know what I have done to you? ¹³"You call Me Teacher and Lord; and you are right, for so I am. ¹⁴"If I then, the Lord and the Teacher, washed your feet, you also ought to wash one another's feet. ¹⁵"For I gave you an example that you also should do as I did to you. ¹⁶"Truly, truly, I say to you, a slave is not greater than his master, nor is one who is sent greater than the one who sent him. ¹⁷"If you know these things, you are blessed if you do them. . . ."

· ·

³⁴"A new commandment I give to you, that you love one another, even as I have loved you, that you also love one another. ³⁵"By this all men will know that you are My disciples, if you have love for one another."

his "hour" had come. Throughout his Gospel, John develops this theme of Jesus' hour. The "hour" represents Jesus upcoming death, in which his entire ministry would be fulfilled. During Jesus' first miracle, he told his mother that his "hour" had not yet come (2:4). In Jesus' prayer to the Father, he clearly stated, "Father, the hour has come" (17:1).

John 13 is a beautiful representation of the sacrificial nature of Jesus' death. "He loved them to the end" (13:1) has a double meaning. The NIV says, "He now showed them the full extent of this love" (13:1, NIV), but it can also mean Jesus loved them until the conclusion of his earthly ministry.

Verse 2 casts a shadow over the entire scene. The devil planted thoughts of betrayal into the heart of Judas. This act does not negate Judas's freedom of choice; it only emphasizes the origin of the idea. Judas chose to listen to Satan. John has already given us a glimpse of Judas's intent (12:4–6), and we see more about this in 13:18–30.

How would you treat someone if you knew the person was planning on betraying you?

Jesus had full knowledge of Judas's plans. Yet, the influence of Satan did not deter Jesus from his purpose. Against this backdrop of evil and darkness, the light of Jesus shines even more brightly. Jesus continued to show his love for Judas right up until the end. How would you treat someone if you knew the person was planning on betraying you?

The Gospel of John makes clear Jesus' total control of the situation. The presence of Judas underscores the incredible act of service Jesus performed when he washed the disciples' feet. Jesus knew that Judas had already made plans to betray him, and yet Jesus washed Judas's feet.

Jesus knew where he came from and where he was going. He knew the role of Satan in the events about to unfold; yet Jesus also knew that Satan could not thwart his Father's purpose.

The meal apparently had begun already when Jesus got up. During a feast such as this, the guests reclined on couches with their heads facing the center and their feet behind them. The guests leaned on their left elbow and ate with their right hand. The place of honor was a couch in the center of the room. The person in the very center was the most honored, with the positions to his right and left next in importance.

The question of who would sit beside Jesus may have been what prompted an argument among the disciples about who would be the greatest (see Luke 22:24–30), or the disciples may have been arguing about who should wash the feet of the other disciples. If the disciples had realized the events that were about to take place, the source of the disagreement would not have mattered. Jesus was thinking about his death on the cross, and his disciples were arguing about insignificant details! If they had recognized the shadow of death, how much would it have changed their perspectives?

The custom was for the host to provide a slave or servant to wash the feet of his guests. Because Jesus did not have such a person, nobody was available to perform this service. The basin of water and the towel had been present all along. The disciples must have known about the custom. Were they so busy arguing that they did not notice Jesus when he got up? Any of the disciples would have been hon-

Jesus knew where he came from and where he was going.

ored to wash Jesus' feet; it was their fellow disciples whom they did not want to serve. Not one of them wanted to imply that he was any less important than the others.

How shocked the disciples must have been when Jesus laid aside his outer garments, took a towel, and wrapped it around his waist. Wrapping the towel allowed Jesus to use both hands, while underscoring the lowly nature of the task he was about to perform. Thus Jesus' appearance resembled the way a slave would dress. We tend to be so familiar with the story that we miss the absurdity of the moment. How it must have jolted the disciples to see their Lord appearing and acting like a slave!

Peter Refuses (13:6–11)

Peter just didn't get it. He allowed the typical Jewish views of Messiah to cloud his vision. In Peter's eyes, the Messiah was supposed to be an

Washing Feet

The custom of washing the feet of guests during biblical times was important. The most obvious reason was personal hygiene. The roads were dusty during the dry season and muddy following heavy rains. The sandals worn by most travelers had only one or two straps across the top of the foot. Following miles and miles of walking, the feet of travelers would be extremely dirty. Most hosts would have a servant wash the feet of their guests as a gesture of hospitality. The lowliest servant normally performed this service, although a host might provide it for his guests if no servant was available. By law, Jewish slaves or servants could not be required to wash feet because it was considered so degrading. (Gentile slaves or servants could be required to perform this function.)

A religious significance was also attached to footwashing. Custom dictated that guests take a bath prior to the Passover, and washing the feet of the guests was also a requirement for the feast.

Meeting Needs

As I write this lesson, a friend of mine is dealing with some monumental concerns. Her husband has had cancer for two years and is not doing well. They have five children and live in a small apartment. The family's income doesn't even come close to covering their bills. How would you and your church serve this family during this time of need?

Can you think of a family in your church who has some serious needs nobody seems to be meeting? What do you think should be done? What do you think *you* should do?

exalted ruler! The role Jesus was about to fulfill as the Suffering Servant just did not square with Peter's hopes and dreams for Jesus. Mark 8:31–35 tells of a time when Peter rebuked Jesus for talking about suffering. Jesus reacted very strongly because he realized that the entire purpose of his coming to earth was to suffer for the sins of humanity. The other disciples were no different; they just relied on Peter to express what everyone else was thinking.

> *. . . In order for the church to function as Jesus intended, we must be willing to offer as well as receive acts of service from one another.*

When it was Peter's turn to have his feet washed, he protested. While Jesus washed the feet of other disciples, Peter's head must have been spinning. Impulsive and outspoken as usual, Peter blurted out a protest. In current language it might have been something like, *Master, no way will I let you wash my feet—ever!*

Jesus' reply has a symbolic meaning. If Peter did not allow the Lord to wash his feet, Jesus said, "You have no part with Me" (John 13:8). Washing the disciples' feet is symbolic of Jesus' sacrificial death for all on the cross. Thus, if Peter did not allow Jesus to wash his feet, he was rejecting the death of Jesus as well.

Peter seemed to understand, but he went overboard. In his enthusiasm, he asked Jesus to wash his hands and head as well.

Jesus must have been amused at this outburst from his disciple. Jesus good-naturedly replied that if one has taken a bath, it is only one's feet that need to be washed.

Peter still didn't really grasp the message Jesus was trying to teach. The disciples were already clean because of their relationship to Jesus, not because of any ritual footwashing or anointing. Yet Jesus added a word of caution, that one of them was not "clean" (13:10). Throughout the story, John wanted to remind his readers of what was coming. Jesus was going to be betrayed by one of his own disciples.

The Meaning (13:12–17)

Jesus put his outer clothing back on and returned to his position as the teacher and leader. Jesus made sure that the disciples caught his intended meaning. In case they didn't understand, he spelled it out for them. He acknowledged that he was worthy of the honor they showed by calling him "Teacher and "Lord." Instead of saying, *Because I have washed your feet, now you wash mine*, Jesus turned the thought around. Now the disciples "ought to wash one another's feet" (13:14).

The message is symbolic. Because Jesus accepted the role of servant to his disciples, how much more should they be willing to serve one another! Any of the disciples would have gladly washed Jesus' feet, but they were completely unwilling to perform the service for their fellow disciples. Recall how Luke gives a glimpse of what the disciples were thinking about when he described the argument about who was the greatest among the Twelve (Luke 22:24–30). None of them doubted Jesus' position of authority. They were worried about their own positions within his kingdom.

Not one of them wanted to imply that he was any less important than the others.

Jesus showed the nature of his kingdom. The leaders in the kingdom of God would be those who were willing to take a position of servitude. The hierarchy of the world is thus turned completely around. Traditional roles are totally crushed. So a radical change must occur. Those at the top should take their positions at the bottom. If one wants to be truly great in this new order, one must first learn how to serve.

A New Commandment (13:34–35)

The Greek word translated "new" in verse 34 means *something different, totally unique, without equal.* This "new commandment" may not sound like anything special. Many leaders want their followers to love one another. The *Torah* contains a command for Jews to love their neighbors (Leviticus 19:18). Jesus gave a hint of this new commandment in Matthew 22:35–40. When a lawyer asked Jesus which of the commandments was the most important, Jesus said that love for God is the first commandment. Another mandate Jesus put right beside love for God was love for our neighbor.

Jesus' ministry gives this love a whole new meaning. The difference is that Jesus has set the example. "Love one another *as I have loved you*" (John 13:34, italics for emphasis). Throughout Jesus' ministry, Jesus exhibited a love that cares for the needs of the individual. The servant nature of Jesus finds its ultimate fulfillment in his death. In light of what Jesus had just done in washing the feet of the disciples, he gave them (and us) a glimpse of the love he expects.

If one wants to be truly great in this new order, one must first learn how to serve.

We do not love one another based on money or position. Rather we love one another because we are all one body. That means the lowliest in the eyes of the world should receive just as much love as the most revered leaders! Jesus said the world will know that we are his disciples if we have this kind of love for one another. The world does not understand this love, because the love the world gives is based on authority and position.

Conclusion

Jesus chose the final hours before his death to illustrate his love for his disciples. Rejection of Jesus' act of service means rejecting the entire ministry of the Lord. In order to follow Jesus' example as a servant leader, we must first receive the gift of his sacrificial love through his death on the cross. Only then can we have the power and ability to follow Jesus in loving others.

Jesus said the world will know that we are his disciples if we have this kind of love for one another.

Jesus' washing the feet of his followers gives us a powerful picture of the way we are to treat one another in the church. Washing someone's feet is a very intimate experience. Because of this, we form a deep personal connection with the other individual. We need this type of involvement in one another's lives to truly exhibit the characteristics of Christ's kingdom here on earth.

The love Jesus showed us on the cross is the same love we are called on to exhibit on a daily basis to our fellow believers. Just as Peter did not want to accept Jesus' act of service, it can sometimes be hard for us to accept the help of fellow believers. We live in a very independent society, and it is hard for us to admit that we need anything. Yet in order for the church to function as Jesus intended, we must be willing to offer as well as receive acts of service from one another.

QUESTIONS

1. Read Philippians 2:5–11 and consider Jesus' act in John 13 in light of that passage. What do both of these passages reveal about the character of Jesus?

2. What disagreements over position or responsibility might be creating strife in your church or your relationships? How would it change the situation if you decided to act out of service to others instead of pride and ambition?

3. What are some creative ways you can serve fellow believers this week?

4. How can we become more deeply involved in one another's lives so that we can serve one another in a personal manner?

5. Is it sometimes easier to give money than to truly serve others sacrificially? Why or why not?

Focal Text

John 14:1–11,
15–18, 25–27

Background

John 14:1–31

Main Idea

Jesus offers assurance
that we are not alone
and that he will provide
for us forever.

Question to Explore

How can we face a world
of change and loss?

Study Aim

To affirm that we can find assurance in
Christ for facing life's difficulties

Study and Action Emphases

- Affirm the Bible as our authoritative guide for
  life and ministry
- Share the gospel with all people
- Develop a growing, vibrant faith

LESSON EIGHT

Rest Assured

Quick Read

Jesus provides the Holy Spirit to reassure and
comfort us during the times we feel deserted.

When I was in college, the pastor of our church resigned to take a position at another church. Most people in the church were shocked. He was a very popular pastor. Too, if any major problems existed in the church, I wasn't aware of them. His last sermon was designed to prepare the church to accept the new leadership that would inevitably come. A feeling of trepidation was apparent in the room, but the overwhelming view expressed by members was a sense of joy for his ministry and anticipation of the continued ministry he would have with a new congregation. The Holy Spirit gave us peace that God was in control, and we looked forward to the future.

When Jesus gave his final address to his disciples, they had only the promise of the Holy Spirit. They were not sure what Jesus was talking about. Their whole world was about to change. Up to this point, the twelve men from Galilee had enjoyed intimate fellowship with the most profound Teacher in the history of the world. Jesus had taught, counseled, and protected them and had put their minds at ease. An incredible future was before them, but they did not see it.

Jesus stood in their midst talking about leaving. He was going to be betrayed by one of his own disciples. How could this be? What would their future look like after Jesus was gone? Were all their hopes and dreams about to be crushed by the cruel arm of Rome?

I Will Prepare a Place for You (14:1–7)

Jesus had told his disciples that one of them would betray him (John 13:18, 21) and that he was going away (13:33–36). They were naturally confused and upset. They did not really understand who Jesus was or what his mission here on earth was. The disciples' entire world was in turmoil. Their leader was about to go away, and they did not understand.

Jesus wanted to reassure them before he left. He knew what they were about to endure. "Do not let your heart be troubled" means more than telling them not to worry. The word "troubled" conveys the idea of deep emotion. This is the same word used to describe Jesus' mood when he saw Mary crying over the death of Lazarus (11:33), when he contemplated the cross (12:27), and when he told the disciples Judas would betray him (13:21).

Jesus did not simply tell them not to be troubled, though. The next words of Jesus told them how to overcome their emotions and stand firm

John 14:1–11, 15–18, 25–27

[1]"Do not let your heart be troubled; believe in God, believe also in Me. [2]"In My Father's house are many dwelling places; if it were not so, I would have told you; for I go to prepare a place for you. [3]"If I go and prepare a place for you, I will come again and receive you to Myself, that where I am, there you may be also. [4]"And you know the way where I am going." [5]Thomas said to Him, "Lord, we do not know where You are going, how do we know the way?" [6]Jesus said to him, "I am the way, and the truth, and the life; no one comes to the Father but through Me.

[7]"If you had known Me, you would have known My Father also; from now on you know Him, and have seen Him."

[8]Philip said to Him, "Lord, show us the Father, and it is enough for us." [9]Jesus said to him, "Have I been so long with you, and yet you have not come to know Me, Philip? He who has seen Me has seen the Father; how can you say, 'Show us the Father'? [10]"Do you not believe that I am in the Father, and the Father is in Me? The words that I say to you I do not speak on My own initiative, but the Father abiding in Me does His works. [11]"Believe Me that I am in the Father and the Father is in Me; otherwise believe because of the works themselves.

.   .   .   .

[15]"If you love Me, you will keep My commandments.

[16]"I will ask the Father, and He will give you another Helper, that He may be with you forever; [17]that is the Spirit of truth, whom the world cannot receive, because it does not see Him or know Him, but you know Him because He abides with you and will be in you.

[18]"I will not leave you as orphans; I will come to you.

.   .   .   .

[25]"These things I have spoken to you while abiding with you. [26]"But the Helper, the Holy Spirit, whom the Father will send in My name, He will teach you all things, and bring to your remembrance all that I said to you. [27]"Peace I leave with you; My peace I give to you; not as the world gives do I give to you. Do not let your heart be troubled, nor let it be fearful."

in the midst of the turmoil. The next portion can be a statement, *You believe in God*, or a command, *Believe in God*. I think that the latter is a better translation. The disciples believed in God, but their faith was about to be severely tested. Jesus thus instructed them, *Have faith that the Father is in control and wants what is best for you.*

"Believe also in Me" is a strange instruction coming from someone who knew he was going to die. How does one have faith in a dead man? He was about to be humiliated publicly and nailed to a criminal's cross. How could they continue to trust Jesus through the coming days? Jesus gave them a glimpse of his deity in this passage. Jesus demanded a faith from the disciples equal to their faith in God! Jesus knew the way the story would end. He would be raised from the dead and be alive for all eternity! The key to the disciples' survival through all the trials to come was linked to their belief in the Father and the Son.

What would their future look like after Jesus was gone?

Jesus publicly mentioned his departure in John 7:33–34 and again in 8:21, but he did not say where he was going. He said only that they could not come. Now the reason for the departure was made clear. Jesus was going to his Father's house to prepare for the arrival of the disciples. The identification with God is apparent throughout this passage. The Father demanded trust; Jesus demanded trust. His return to the Father's house was the return of the beloved Son, the heir to all the Father owns. The word "dwelling places," translated "mansions" in the King James Version, is the word for *a place to stay*. Because it is in the Father's house, *suites, rooms,* or *apartments* may convey the meaning best. The image is one of hospitality and welcome. Just think of the encouragement of that concept, to be forever with the Lord in the Father's house!

An incredible future was before them, but they did not see it.

Jesus was going to make a place ready for them. The very act of Jesus' departure was the way in which he would prepare the place. His death on the cross makes our journey to the Father's house a possibility. Jesus' victorious return to God is the reason disciples do not need to be afraid. Jesus' death is not a tragedy; rather it is a victory.

The conclusion to this section seems to be a logical progression. If Jesus was going to prepare a place, he would return to take them with him. Many see this as a clear reference to the Second Coming of Jesus. The tense of the verb translated "will come" suggests a process as well as a single act. Therefore, it can also be interpreted to mean that as a believer dies, Jesus takes him or her to heaven. Either way, the certainty is that Jesus will return for his own so that we can be with him in eternity. The culmination of history is in Jesus' triumphant return.

If the disciples knew where Jesus was going, why did he have to return to take them with him? Couldn't they simply follow? This must have been the way Thomas was thinking in verse 5. Jesus must have smiled when he said that they knew the way. The way for Jesus was the way of a sacrificial death on a cross, the way of suffering. He knew they did not understand what he was saying. Thomas's reply made that very clear. Thomas asked, *How could we know the way when we don't even know where you are going?* Jesus' listeners often failed to understand what Jesus was talking about (see 3:4, 9; 4:11–12, 15; 6:34; 13:9). In the Gospel of John, this confusion gave Jesus a chance to clarify what he meant. It also gives us some important insights into Jesus' purpose. Thomas was only a spokesman for the others. None of them seemed to know Jesus' identity or his purpose. They were unwilling to give up the idea of Jesus as an earthly ruler; therefore the thought of his suffering and death was inconceivable.

> *The key to the disciples' survival through all the trials to come was linked to their belief in the Father and the Son.*

Jesus' declaration that he is "the way, and the truth, and the life" is a summary of his life and the reason he came to earth. Jesus came to earth to show us a picture of God. Through Jesus "the Word became flesh" (1:14). God became a human being, and people are reconciled to God because of Jesus' life and death. Jesus is the Only Son, whom God gave to save the world (3:16). For Jesus, the way to the Father was death. For us, the

The Holy Spirit, Our Helper

John 14—16 contains five sayings about the Holy Spirit (14:15–17, 26; 15:26; 16:7–11, 13–15). The word "Helper" or "Comforter" (KJV) is from the Greek word *paraclete* (14:16). John is the only author in the New Testament to use this term for the Holy Sprit. This term literally means *one who is called alongside*, and it normally refers to a defender in a courtroom, an advocate before the court. Although often used as a legal term, the word can also have the sense of someone defending another in public. Jesus said he was sending "another" Helper, meaning that up to this point in time, Jesus had been their defender (14:16).

The gift of the Holy Spirit replaced Jesus' physical presence with the disciples. Jesus probably came to the disciples' aid many times while he was with them, just as one would expect from a leader. God sent the Holy Spirit because of Jesus' love and concern for the disciples, not because they earned it. Just as salvation itself is a gift, the coming of the Holy Spirit is also a gift.

way to the Father is only through the death of Jesus. Jesus did not merely *show* us a way to God; rather Jesus *is* the only way to God. Too, Jesus is "the truth." "The way" and "the truth" are not abstract. They are alive in the person of Jesus Christ. He is not a set of truths to be studied and copied. The truth can be discovered only through a personal relationship with Jesus. Also, Jesus is "the life." Real life can be achieved only through union with God through the Son, Jesus.

> The truth can be discovered only through a personal relationship with Jesus.

This statement about Jesus' being "the way, and the truth, and the life" is full of irony. The "way" of Jesus was the way of a cross, the death of a common criminal. The "truth" is revealed in One who was convicted because of lying witnesses, and his own people did not believe him. The "life" of Jesus was about to be taken from him, and Jesus' lifeless body would soon be hanging on the cross.

Show Us the Way (14:8–11)

Poor Philip! He was really trying to grasp what Jesus was saying! He wanted to please Jesus, and he was trying to believe. *Just show us the Father and we'll understand better*, he seemed to say. The disciples didn't understand the life of faith. They were still living in an empirical world that requires visible evidence. *Just give us something solid to hold on to!* Jesus' patience must have yielded to a touch of disappointment in his reply. He had been with them for three years and they still didn't get it! How many times do we want proof from Jesus? *Just show me, Lord*, is often the cry of my heart instead of *Give me more faith*.

> Real life can be achieved only through union with God through the Son, Jesus.

Jesus is so intimately related to God that the disciples had seen God because they had seen Jesus. This is part of the mystery of the Trinity: Jesus and God are separate and yet so closely intertwined that they are also one. The unity that exists between the Father and the Son cannot be fully expressed in our language. John wanted to make sure his readers understood this. "The Word was with God, and the Word was God" (1:1), and "the Word became flesh" (1:14). The Father directed Jesus throughout his ministry, working through him.

The Spirit of Truth (14:15–18)

If we love Jesus, we will keep his commandments. What are Jesus' commands? This thought will be developed more fully in the next lesson, on John 15, where Jesus speaks of the command to "love one another" (15:12). When we truly follow Jesus and seek to obey him, we love one another and the Holy Spirit abides within us.

Jesus said he is "the truth" (14:6). Now Jesus promised to send "the Spirit of truth" (14:17). Jesus told them that the Spirit will "guide you into all the truth" (16:13). John 14:17 is one instance in which the Spirit seems so closely connected with Jesus that they appear almost interchangeable. The Holy Spirit will never contradict Jesus' words, because the truth cannot conflict with itself. The world cannot know the Holy Spirit because the world is in rebellion to God. If people do not recognize Jesus, how can they know the Holy Spirit sent by Jesus?

> *When we truly follow Jesus and seek to obey him, we love one another and the Holy Spirit abides within us.*

Jesus promised to "come to" the disciples (14:18). This statement could refer to the appearances of Jesus following the resurrection, or it could refer to the coming of the Holy Spirit. Either idea is possible, but I think it refers to the coming of the Holy Spirit. Jesus promised not to leave the disciples as "orphans." The word can mean a child who has lost his or her parents, but it can refer also to a group of disciples who have lost their teacher. Jesus would come back to them after his resurrection, but his abiding presence would remain with them through the Holy Spirit.

I Give You My Peace (14:25–27)

Jesus knew that the disciples would not remember all the things he taught them while he was with them. Jesus reassured them that the Holy Spirit would help them remember what he said, and would continue to teach them.

The disciples' world was reeling as they tried to comprehend all Jesus was saying to them. They were self-absorbed, and they were worrying about what would happen to them without their leader. Jesus reassured them that after he was gone, the Holy Spirit would not only help them

Characteristics of the Holy Spirit

- Sent by the Father (John 14:16, 26; 15:26) and the Son (16:7–8)
- Not known by the world (14:17)
- Abides within us (14:17)
- Teaches and helps us remember Jesus' teachings (14:26)
- Points to and glorifies Christ (15:26; 16:14)
- Convicts the world (16:8)
- Reveals the truth (16:13–14)

remember but also would teach them what Jesus meant during the lifetime Jesus spent with them.

Jesus must have sensed that they were still disturbed over what was about to happen. Verse 27 has been used many times to comfort people in similar times of unrest and emotional turmoil. This promise of peace resonates with us, especially during difficult times. The peace the world gives is fragile and temporary. The peace of Jesus is secure and enduring.

Holy Spirit (15:26; 16:7–11, 13–15)

The Holy Spirit is sent by the Father in the Son's name and at the request of the Son (14:16, 26; 15:26; 16:7–8). The Holy Spirit is Christ's representative in the world. Although the disciples were apprehensive and anxious about the future, Jesus reassured them that his departure was for their good. We can see that the death of Jesus was necessary because of the need for atonement of sins. What is more difficult for us to fathom is that the disciples were somehow better off without Jesus' physical presence in their midst (16:7). After Jesus was gone, the Holy Spirit came to minister to the disciples. Jesus was limited to time and space while he was on the earth. The Holy Spirit does not experience the same limitations because he abides within every believer (14:17).

This promise of peace resonates with us, especially during difficult times.

The Holy Spirit continues Jesus' work of teaching the disciples (14:26) and convicting the world (16:8–11). In addition to the Holy Spirit's role as teacher, the Holy Spirit also helped the disciples remember the lessons

Jesus had taught them while he was with them (14:26). Satan was judged when Jesus died on the cross (16:11). The world is judged because the world is under Satan's rule (16:11). The role of the Holy Spirit is to bring those in the world under conviction, so that they may realize their sin and turn to Jesus as their Savior.

QUESTIONS

1. How does Jesus' promise of peace relate to someone who has just lost a spouse? a child?

2. Can we keep the commands of Jesus without being empowered by the Holy Spirit? Why or why not?

3. What do you think Jesus meant in John 14:20, where he said, "I am in My Father, and you in Me, and I in you?"

4. According to John 14:13, what is the purpose of answered prayer? What would our world look like if we really believed and put into practice Jesus' statement in verses 13–14?

Focal Text

John 15:1–17

Background

John 15—16

Main Idea

Staying united to Jesus leads to being faithful in serving him, a quality that marks genuine followers of Jesus.

Question to Explore

Is an unproductive Christian a contradiction in terms?

Study Aim

To evaluate my life by how faithful I am in serving Jesus

Study and Action Emphases

- Affirm the Bible as our authoritative guide for life and ministry
- Share the gospel with all people
- Develop a growing, vibrant faith
- Obey and serve Jesus by meeting physical, spiritual, and emotional needs
- Equip people for servant leadership

LESSON NINE

Stay United to Jesus

Quick Read

When we truly abide in Jesus, we depend on him for our needs. We will obey Jesus' commandments out of our love for him.

The last few years my family has enjoyed having a vegetable garden in our yard. I love the taste of homegrown tomatoes. I heard someone say that even ants can tell the difference between vine-ripened tomatoes and those that are store-bought. I tried the experiment and was amazed! If you slice a vine-ripened tomato and place it next to a cut, store-bought tomato, the ants will cover the one that is homegrown and leave the other alone! The reason is that many of the nutrients in the tomato do not appear until it ripens on the vine. Just as the tomato depends on the vine for the fruit to grow and develop, we as Christians are called on to rely on Jesus for our fruitfulness.

John 15:1–17

[1]"I am the true vine, and My Father is the vinedresser. [2]"Every branch in Me that does not bear fruit, He takes away; and every branch that bears fruit, He prunes it so that it may bear more fruit. [3]"You are already clean because of the word which I have spoken to you. [4]"Abide in Me, and I in you. As the branch cannot bear fruit of itself unless it abides in the vine, so neither can you unless you abide in Me. [5]"I am the vine, you are the branches; he who abides in Me and I in him, he bears much fruit, for apart from Me you can do nothing. [6]"If anyone does not abide in Me, he is thrown away as a branch and dries up; and they gather them, and cast them into the fire and they are burned. [7]"If you abide in Me, and My words abide in you, ask whatever you wish, and it will be done for you. [8]"My Father is glorified by this, that you bear much fruit, and so prove to be My disciples. [9]"Just as the Father has loved Me, I have also loved you; abide in My love. [10]"If you keep My commandments, you will abide in My love; just as I have kept My Father's commandments and abide in His love. [11]"These things I have spoken to you so that My joy may be in you, and that your joy may be made full.

[12]"This is My commandment, that you love one another, just as I have loved you. [13]"Greater love has no one than this, that one lay down his life for his friends. [14]"You are My friends if you do what I command you. [15]"No longer do I call you slaves, for the slave does not know what his master is doing; but I have called you friends, for all things that I have heard from My Father I have made known to you. [16]"You did not choose Me but I chose you, and appointed you that you would go and bear fruit, and that your fruit would remain, so that whatever you ask of the Father in My name He may give to you. [17]"This I command you, that you love one another."

Background

Isaiah 5 in the Old Testament uses the imagery of a vine or a vineyard to represent the Jews as God's covenant people. God planted and tended the vine, but the vine failed to produce fruit as God intended. Jesus used the fruit of the vine in the Last Supper to represent his blood that was poured out for all people.

Jesus changed the metaphor in John 15 to represent to his disciples the reality of their relationship with him that would continue even after his death. His final instructions to his disciples just before his death include this picture of what that relationship with him should look like after he was gone.

"Abide In Me" (15:1–9)

Jesus used the language of the Old Testament to proclaim the arrival of a new era. The old covenant is obsolete; this is the age of the new covenant. Yet this new covenant is, in a sense, a continuation of the old. The true vine, the Redeemer of humanity, is the One who transforms the people of God into a new priesthood.

> *. . . We as Christians are called on to rely on Jesus for our fruitfulness.*

The nation of Israel had failed in its mission. God had chosen the nation of Israel to be a nation set apart to honor him. They were to be a light to all the other nations (see Isaiah 42:6). But they continually rejected God and his purposes.

Now Jesus proclaimed that he is the only true vine and his disciples are the branches. In the Old Testament analogy, the vine is judged because of its failure to produce fruit. Jesus shifted the image so that the vine is no longer an institution (the vine is Jesus, not the church), and the branches are now judged because of failure to produce fruit.

Two types of branches exist: those that bear fruit, and those that do not. There is no middle ground. The branches that do not bear fruit are taken away, and the ones that bear fruit are pruned so that they will bear even more fruit.

Notice that the good branches produce fruit without any effort on their part. Bearing fruit is a natural byproduct of a healthy branch. When a person is united to Jesus, it is unavoidable that the person will begin to bear fruit. Obviously, the fruit-bearing branches represent true Christians. What is not so obvious is who the branches that do not bear fruit represent.

Two differing interpretations have been suggested. Some think the non-producing branches represent a group of Christians. If this is the case, why are they cast into the fire? The language seems to represent something that is useless: "He is thrown away as a branch, and dries up; and they gather them, and cast them into the fire and they are burned" (John 15:6). Certainly this language causes the reader to think of judgment, even of hell.

The other interpretation is that the branches represent people who seem to be Christian but are not really part of the faith. Jesus was speaking to the eleven disciples who remained after Judas left to betray Jesus. The sudden departure of Judas was still fresh in all of their minds. After washing their feet, Jesus had told the disciples that they were "clean," but not all of them (13:10). In the prayer recorded in John 17, Jesus said that he protected all of those the Father gave to him, except "the son of perdition," referring to Judas (17:12). Judas represents all those who seem to be followers of Jesus but are never truly part of his own. Judas was one of the original Twelve, and yet he was never a part of them.

Jesus demands obedience as a condition to maintaining a right relationship with him.

The branches that remain are pruned so they can produce more fruit. If the vinedresser does not take good care of the vine, the amount of fruit produced will greatly diminish.

The disciples were about to be severely tested in their faith. The trials they were about to endure were part of God's pruning process. The purpose of the pruning is always to bring greater productivity. God uses circumstances in our lives to help us produce more fruit. The trials we face should not be viewed as punishment, but as God's loving hand stretching us to become the people God wants us to be.

Only through a life of dependence on Jesus can we truly be Jesus' disciples.

Verse 3 contains a play on words that does not carry over into the English. The word translated "prunes" in verse 2 is a form of the same word translated "clean" in verse 3. Jesus said the disciples were already "clean," a reference to his words in John 13:10. There he told them that they were clean, but "not all" of them. The disciples were clean because Jesus had poured out his life into them and they had responded. Because Judas had rejected Jesus, he was not "clean."

Because of our heritage as Americans, many of us exhibit a fierce independence that does not like to admit we need anyone else. Many even consider needing anyone else to be a sign of weakness. This sense of independence is foreign to a life of discipleship. Without a life of dependence on the Lord, we are fruitless, and our lives become futile.

The promise to answer our prayers applies only when our desires are in line with God's divine purpose.

Moreover, a branch does not have to work to produce fruit. In the same manner, the inevitable result of abiding in Christ is that we bear fruit. Working on our own does not produce the desired results.

Furthermore, a branch of a vine that is not productive is useless. Branches of a tree can have various different uses, but the branches of a vine are too soft to be useful. So they are thrown into the fire (15:6).

The relationship between Jesus and his followers mirrors his relationship with the Father. Jesus loves his disciples in the same way that God the Father loves the Son.

Jesus demands obedience as a condition to maintaining a right relationship with him. Sometimes we tend to think we can live the Christian life without remaining in Christ, that we just do it better when we rely on Him. Jesus rejects this thought. He proclaims, "Apart from Me, you can do nothing" (15:5). The reality is that the branches cannot even begin to survive without complete and total reliance on the vine for their sustenance.

The relationship between Jesus and the Father was marked by obedience. Jesus took great delight in doing exactly what the Father asked of

Bearing Fruit

What is the fruit of a disciple? I have heard many pastors say, "The fruit of a Christian is another Christian." Although this sounds good, finding solid scriptural basis for it is difficult if not impossible. Throughout his final words to his disciples, Jesus repeatedly challenged them to love one another (John 13:34; 15:10, 12, 17). The fruit of true followers of Jesus is manifested in this love.

The love Jesus requires is different from the love the world shows. We are to love others as Jesus loved us. Jesus loved his disciples by washing their feet (one of the most menial tasks of the day, 13:1–17), and by laying down his life for them. That type of love is possible only as we remain in Jesus, the vine, and allow Jesus' love to flow through us.

him. Can you imagine Jesus negotiating with God for a lesser standard of behavior? In the same way, our greatest joy should be related directly to our relationship with Jesus and our wholehearted commitment to do what Jesus asks. We do not have the right to question or try to negotiate the terms of obedience.

The purpose of our bearing fruit is that the Father is glorified (15:8). Glorifying God was the supreme purpose of Jesus' life, and it should be our goal as well. If you do not have a desire to follow Jesus' leading in your life, you should seriously consider whether you are truly part of Jesus' family. When we are truly abiding in Jesus, we are miserable when we don't follow him. That doesn't mean we don't ever sin, but it means that when we do sin, we feel guilty.

> *When a person is united to Jesus, it is unavoidable that the person will begin to bear fruit.*

Notice it is Jesus, not the church, who is the vine. Our purpose and power does not come through membership in an organization but through a living relationship with God himself, expressed in the person of the Son. Christianity is all about this relationship, not about adhering to a set of rules and regulations about how one should live.

True Christianity is more than living a good life and believing the right doctrine. Without a supernatural union with Christ, we may be religious, but not Christian. Only through a life of dependence on Jesus can we truly be Jesus' disciples.

Verse 7 is not a magical formula we can use to make sure all our prayers are answered as we want them to be answered. When we are truly abiding in Jesus, and Jesus is abiding in us, our desires will be in line with Jesus' desires. If we look at the relationship between Jesus and the Father, we see how everything Jesus wanted was in complete harmony with God's plan and purpose. To pray for something not in line with God's purposes would have been impossible for Jesus. When we pray for our selfish wants and desires, God does not honor our requests. The promise to answer our prayers applies only when our desires are in line with God's divine purpose.

The Love Commandment (15:10–17)

Jesus repeated the directive that the disciples were to "love one another" (15:12). The verse is very similar to 13:34. Just as a good teacher repeats

Case Study

You have a co-worker who is a Christian of another denomination. She repeatedly tries to convince you that her denomination is right, and you should join her church. You work closely with her and do not want to cause strife in the office. How can you respond in a loving manner?

the important lessons, Jesus the Teacher wanted to make sure the disciples understood the significance of this command. He asked the disciples to "love one another, just as I have loved you" (15:12). He had showed them how to love one another when he washed their feet (John 13). Now Jesus was looking forward to the ultimate act of love in his sacrificial death.

Working on our own does not produce the results we desire.

So should I be willing to serve other people graciously, in such a lowly manner, and then be willing to die for them? How can anyone live up to such a standard? Yet that is exactly what the Lord expects of his followers. The only way this kind of life is possible is through our willingness to remain connected to Jesus and to allow Jesus' life to flow through us. As we are obedient to Jesus, we become more like Jesus, and our pride and ambition vanish in the light of Jesus' grace and mercy.

Jesus now referred to the disciples as "My friends" (15:14). Jesus had one qualification for his disciples if they wanted to be considered his friends. They must "do what I command you" (15:14). Jesus' relationship to his disciples is not like their relationship to one another. Jesus is still the leader, and the cost of following Jesus is full obedience.

Without a life of dependence on the Lord, we are fruitless, and our lives become futile.

If we do as Jesus commands, we are Jesus' friends (15:14). The logical progression is that if we do not follow Jesus' directives, we are Jesus' enemies, or at the very least, we are not Jesus' friends. A halfhearted, shallow commitment is not a possibility. All or nothing. We are, or we are not. There is no in-between. The branch either bears fruit, or it does not. Those that do not bear fruit are not tolerated. Sooner or later, the vinedresser will come and cast them into the fire.

The distinction between slaves and friends is profound. The outsider may not be able to tell the difference. Obedience looks the same whether it is the slave or the friend. If I am your closest friend, I may do what you want me to do because I want to please you. Of course, if I were your slave, I would still do what you want me to do. The difference is not in the actions, but in the motivation. The friend wants to please and acts out of love, but the slave is afraid of the penalty of not obeying. The same is true of our relationship with Jesus. If we are obeying because we are afraid of what will happen if we don't, we are acting more like slaves than like friends. We then will not experience the remarkable freedom Christ gives us because we do not realize how much Christ loves us.

As we are obedient to Jesus, we become more like Jesus, and our pride and ambition vanish in the light of Jesus' grace and mercy.

If I were your slave, you probably would not share your thoughts and intentions with me. However, if we are close friends, everything is shared, and I know what motivates you to do the things you do.

Jesus wants to help his disciples understand this concept. How awesome it is to think that the same God who created me will share his divine purposes with me as a friend! The full revelation of God is made known to us in the person of Jesus Christ.

How radical that concept must have been to the disciples. They refused even to mention the name of God because of God's holiness. They must have wondered how their relationship with God could be so personal.

The status we enjoy as the friends of God is not something we have earned. Jesus did not want his disciples to think that they did something to deserve the incredible gift he had given them. Although Jesus referred to them as friends, this does not mean they were now Jesus' equals. From the very beginning of the relationship, Jesus was in control. Jesus chose them (15:16; see 6:70; 13:18; 15:19). The reason Jesus chose them was not so that they would have something to brag about. Rather Jesus chose them for a life of service to him, so that they would "go and bear fruit" (15:16). The same is true for us.

QUESTIONS

1. How does abiding in Christ affect the way we pray?

2. Who are some modern examples of people who are truly abiding in Christ and have given themselves to him totally?

3. Can you see some examples from your own life where God has "pruned" you to make you more fruitful?

4. How can we help new Christians understand the importance of "abiding in Christ"? How can we help our children? our teenagers?

Main Idea

Jesus prayed for his followers' protection from evil, ministry in the world, and unity with one another and with God and himself.

Question to Explore

What does Jesus want for us?

Study Aim

To decide on at least one way I will allow Jesus' prayer to be answered in my life

Study and Action Emphases

- Affirm the Bible as our authoritative guide for life and ministry
- Share the gospel with all people
- Develop a growing, vibrant faith
- Obey and serve Jesus by meeting physical, spiritual, and emotional needs
- Equip people for servant leadership

LESSON TEN

What Jesus Wants for His Followers

Quick Read

Jesus prayed for the unity, protection, and ministry of his disciples, as well as those who would follow him in the future.

What does Jesus want for his followers—including you and me as well as his first disciples? We can learn much about the answer to this question through the passage of Scripture for this lesson.

Jesus' prayer in John 17 is the longest recorded prayer of Jesus. Immediately before the sacrificial lamb was slain on the altar for the forgiveness of sins, the high priest would offer a prayer for the people. Because of this, many have called this prayer "The High Priestly Prayer." The main themes of the prayer are

(1) Glorification—Jesus prayed that through his sacrifice, God would be glorified.

(2) Protection for his followers—Jesus prayed that his followers would be protected from Satan and from strife that would destroy their unity.

(3) Holiness—Jesus prayed that believers would follow his example.

This prayer provides insight into Jesus' thoughts as he approached his final hours on earth.

John 17

¹Jesus spoke these things; and lifting up His eyes to heaven, He said, "Father, the hour has come; glorify Your Son, that the Son may glorify You, ²even as You gave Him authority over all flesh, that to all whom You have given Him, He may give eternal life. ³"This is eternal life, that they may know You, the only true God, and Jesus Christ whom You have sent. ⁴"I glorified You on the earth, having accomplished the work which You have given Me to do. ⁵"Now, Father, glorify Me together with Yourself, with the glory which I had with You before the world was.

⁶"I have manifested Your name to the men whom You gave Me out of the world; they were Yours and You gave them to Me, and they have kept Your word. ⁷"Now they have come to know that everything You have given Me is from You; ⁸for the words which You gave Me I have given to them; and they received them and truly understood that I came forth from You, and they believed that You sent Me. ⁹"I ask on their behalf; I do not ask on behalf of the world, but of those whom You have given Me; for they are Yours; ¹⁰and all things that are Mine are Yours, and Yours are Mine; and I have been glorified in them. ¹¹"I am no longer in the world; and yet they themselves are in the world, and I come to You. Holy Father,

keep them in Your name, the name which You have given Me, that they may be one even as We are. **12**"While I was with them, I was keeping them in Your name which You have given Me; and I guarded them and not one of them perished but the son of perdition, so that the Scripture would be fulfilled.

13"But now I come to You; and these things I speak in the world so that they may have My joy made full in themselves. **14**"I have given them Your word; and the world has hated them, because they are not of the world, even as I am not of the world. **15**"I do not ask You to take them out of the world, but to keep them from the evil one. **16**"They are not of the world, even as I am not of the world. **17**"Sanctify them in the truth; Your word is truth. **18**"As You sent Me into the world, I also have sent them into the world. **19**"For their sakes I sanctify Myself, that they themselves also may be sanctified in truth.

20"I do not ask on behalf of these alone, but for those also who believe in Me through their word; **21**that they may all be one; even as You, Father, are in Me and I in You, that they also may be in Us, so that the world may believe that You sent Me.

22"The glory which You have given Me I have given to them, that they may be one, just as We are one; **23**I in them and You in Me, that they may be perfected in unity, so that the world may know that You sent Me, and loved them, even as You have loved Me. **24**"Father, I desire that they also, whom You have given Me, be with Me where I am, so that they may see My glory which You have given Me, for You loved Me before the foundation of the world.

25"O righteous Father, although the world has not known You, yet I have known You; and these have known that You sent Me; **26**and I have made Your name known to them, and will make it known, so that the love with which You loved Me may be in them, and I in them."

Father, Glorify Your Son (17:1–5)

Jesus lifted up his eyes toward heaven as he began his prayer. This was a common posture for a Jewish person when praying. The tone of Jesus' prayer is triumphant. He asked for God to glorify him, but the purpose relates back to the Father. Everything Jesus had done was so that God would be glorified, and this was no different. Jesus prayed that his sacrificial death would be pleasing to God. Through Jesus' suffering and death, the grace of God is shown to humanity, and Jesus is restored to the glory he laid aside when he came to earth.

Because of Jesus' obedience, the Father exalted the Son. Jesus' ultimate purpose for coming to earth was about to be fulfilled. Every action had led Jesus to this point.

Through the cross, humanity sees the glory of Christ. John did not view the cross as a disgrace but as the necessary means for Jesus' exaltation. Jesus' death on the cross was no tragedy! Jesus' finest hour, the reason he left heaven, was here. Humanity would be redeemed.

God gave the Son the authority to grant eternal life to all that the Father had given to Jesus. A definition of eternal life follows—"that they may know You, the only true God, and Jesus Christ whom You have sent" (John 17:3). Knowing God is not mere intellectual assent. The word translated "know" implies a personal relationship. Without this relationship with God through Jesus, eternal life is impossible. This is the whole reason Jesus came to earth, to give us an opportunity to know God in an intimate way.

If we are not a part of the family of God, we do not really know God.

I can know who the president of the United States is without really knowing the president. I can meet the president and still not really know the president. The ones with the most intimate knowledge of the president are those in the president's immediate family. It is the same with our relationship to God. If we are not a part of the family of God, we do not really know God. As we become a part of God's family, we are transformed into his likeness.

Jesus said that his mission had been accomplished. Yet the cross still loomed before him. He spoke of it in the past tense because in his mind it was already finished (17:4, 11). He knew he could choose to reject the cross and the suffering. But Jesus' entire life had been devoted to glorifying God, and he would not entertain any thoughts contrary to the Father's will. The decision had already been made. There was no turning back. His mind was set, and he was on his way back home. The final act of obedience would be death as a criminal on a Roman cross.

I Revealed You to My Disciples (17:6–10)

The focus of Jesus' prayer now turns to his disciples. Jesus manifested the name of God by revealing God's nature to the disciples. These are the

Kosmos in the Gospel of John

The word translated "world" (*kosmos*, 17:6) is a major theme in John's Gospel. The word appears often in the first eighteen chapters, including eighteen times in John 17.

"The world" represents all that was created by God. Jesus was sent to the world to reveal the nature of God and to offer salvation. But because the world rejects Jesus, the world rejects its own Creator (see John 1:10).

In contrast to the disciples, the world has not received Jesus' word, has not understood his relationship with the Father, and has not believed that Jesus was sent by God. Because the world rejected Jesus, the world rejected God.

The word normally has a negative connotation, although God still loves the world despite humankind's rejection (3:16). The disciples are in the world, but they are not part of the world (17:14, 16). Jesus prayed for the protection of his disciples because they would remain in this hostile environment.

---

ones God chose to help Jesus carry out his earthly ministry. Although the disciples were immature in their belief and understanding, their commitment to Jesus and his purpose was real. They followed Jesus' leading and sought to obey his commands. Their understanding was growing, and they were beginning to understand the relationship between the Father and the Son. Yet these same men would soon be scattered and would deny their connection to Jesus. Even though they believed in who Jesus was, they were still confused about Jesus' role on earth. When the events of the next few days began to unfold, the disciples were bewildered and confused.

> *Jesus wanted his disciples to be set aside specifically for the purpose of spreading the good news to the unbelieving world.*

Jesus knew that despite the disciples' shortcomings, they would be transformed through the gift of the Holy Spirit. He saw the future loyalty of the disciples and overlooked the brief period of turmoil they were about to experience. Their failure was only a temporary setback, not a permanent rejection. The disciples knew that Jesus was sent by God, and they had seen his dependence on the Father. Even the teachings of Jesus were not his own; they came directly from God (17:8).

The disciples were beginning to understand because Jesus was faithful to deliver the message God gave him. Jesus' message was not mere human words. Rather, Jesus' message was divine words given from the Father. Throughout his final prayer, Jesus emphasized his obedience to God, because Jesus would expect the disciples to display the same allegiance to him that he showed the Father (15:9–10).

Jesus stated that his prayer was not for the entire world, but specifically for his disciples (17:9). Of course Jesus was not indifferent to the world. He had created the world (1:1–3) and had come to earth to save the world (3:16). Still, Jesus placed the emphasis on his followers because it was only through their witness that the world had any hope of salvation. Through their faithfulness and witness, many within the world would be saved.

Jesus' request is really quite simple and can be summed up in one word: unity.

The incredible unity that exists between Jesus and the Father is mentioned in 17:10. Although the Father and Son are two distinct entities, the inseparable unity that binds them together emphasizes the oneness that exists between them. This is the mystery of the Trinity. Father, Son, and Spirit are separate, yet one.

Unify and Protect My Disciples (17:11–19)

In Jewish culture, a name was much more important than in our present culture. In the Old Testament, the name of God was indistinguishable from the power of God. In 17:11, Jesus called on the Father to use his power to protect the disciples and keep them unified. Jesus kept them safe while he was with them, and he was now turning their protection over to the Father. The only exception was Judas, and Jesus was not responsible for Judas's loss. Judas's betrayal of Jesus was part of the plan, but it was Judas's own evil heart that determined his fate.

In verse 11 Jesus said to God, "I come to You." The end of Jesus' earthly ministry was upon him, and Jesus was looking forward to his return to heaven. His divine purpose would soon be accomplished, and the next phase in the plan of redemption was about to unfold.

In verse 13, Jesus gave his purpose for the prayer, so that the disciples "may have My joy made full in themselves" (see also 15:11; 16:24). This joy was not a result of outward circumstances but a deep abiding faith that the Father was in control and all would be accomplished just as God had planned. The time Jesus spent with the disciples on the earth had been for this purpose. When the trials came, Jesus wanted to be sure they would stand firm.

Throughout Jesus' time with the disciples, he had been teaching about God. "I have given them Your word" (17:14) has a dual meaning. Jesus had taught them verbally, but in another sense, his very life as the Word was poured into them (see 1:1–14). It is impossible to separate Jesus' teachings from Jesus' life.

Jesus realized that the disciples' unity with him alienated them from the world (17:14). The world would treat his disciples just as the world treated him. Suffering and even death awaited them.

Jesus prayed for protection from "the evil one," not for deliverance (17:15) out of the world. When we are in the world, we are still in Satan's domain. Too many times, we want to be taken out of the world, away from its worries and problems, instead of asking God to protect us while we are in the world. If God had taken the disciples out of the world, who would have been left to witness to the world?

The whole purpose for unity is to reach a dying world that is lost without Jesus.

Jesus also prayed that the disciples would be sanctified (17:17, 19). The word "sanctified" literally means *to make holy* and thus has the sense of *setting something aside for a specific purpose.* Jesus wanted his disciples to be set aside specifically for the purpose of spreading the good news to the unbelieving world.

Let the World Know (17:20–26)

Jesus now turned to a very popular portion of the prayer because he was praying here for you and me. I can remember as a junior high and high school student how awesome it was for me to think of Jesus praying for me. What I did not realize at the time was that Jesus was not praying just

For Thought, Prayer, and Action

Many Baptist churches have split because of issues large and small. What are some issues that threaten to destroy unity in churches today? What issues are too important to allow for compromise? What can you do to maintain unity within your own church?

for individuals. Rather he was praying for the future church, the believing community. Jesus' request is really quite simple and can be summed up in one word: *unity.*

Yet the intent of Jesus' words has been debated throughout the centuries. Given the many different denominations of Christ's church, what does it mean for us to be one, united, today? It may help to examine the reason Jesus gives for praying for our unity. The first reason is "that the world may believe that You sent me" (17:21). The same reason is stated again in verse 23, and another reason is added to it: "that the world may know that You . . . loved them, even as You have loved Me." These two reasons are directly related to the church's witness in the community. Many commentators focus on what is meant by the unity of the church but miss Jesus' main emphasis. The whole purpose for unity is to reach a dying world that is lost without Jesus. When our focus is on letting the world know who Jesus is and how very much Jesus loves them, unity is a byproduct. We do not have to focus on trying to achieve unity; rather, our focus needs to be on the message of the gospel.

. . . The unity Christ desired for his church has eluded us throughout history.

It may seem that the unity Christ desired for his church has eluded us throughout history. Churches have persecuted each other, and Christians have even killed each other over doctrinal differences. Just open a phone book in any community in this country and you will see many churches from various denominations. Jesus prayed so fervently for unity because he knew the dangers that lay ahead. The Billy Graham crusades were a great example of how denominations could come together for the purpose of reaching people for Christ.

Jesus prayed so fervently for unity because he knew the dangers that lay ahead.

After I graduated from college, I was a member of a church that almost split. The deacons made a decision that many people in the church felt overstepped their authority as church representatives. My own family was split over the issue. My dad was a deacon, and my sisters, my brother, and I felt that the deacons had made a poor decision. My mother stood with the deacons' decision.

I remember the turmoil as I realized that although I greatly respected my parents, I might not always agree with them. Of course I had disagreed with them before, but this was different. This disagreement was more important than a difference of opinion about what to wear to church.

This was an issue that had an impact on relationships within the church and the composition of the church staff. We had to set aside our differences with my parents in order to maintain harmony within the family.

I think this is what having unity within the church means. Yes, we will disagree. Sometimes opposing sides may be incapable of working out an acceptable compromise. Yet we should be able to work through our problems in a Christlike manner and love others throughout the entire process. This kind of unity is not something we can manufacture on our own. The unity Christ prayed for is possible only when people in the church are abiding in Christ and allowing the Holy Spirit to work in their hearts and lives.

The unity Christ prayed for is possible only when people in the church are abiding in Christ and allowing the Holy Spirit to work in their hearts and lives.

QUESTIONS

1. What are some practical guidelines churches can use to work through controversial issues?

2. How can churches cooperate without abandoning their theological diversity?

3. What are some ways we can teach our children to be "in the world" but "not of the world"? How good an example do you think we are setting for them?

4. What are some of the issues we face in our churches today? How can we minister effectively in spite of differences?

Jesus' Passion and Victory

Jesus' *passion* refers to his death and suffering. Jesus showed us how to live, how to focus our lives, and how to die.

Lesson eleven explores the death of Jesus on the cross (John 19). You will discover the incredible focus that Jesus maintained as he moved toward the cross with unrelenting energy. You will learn about Jesus' death sentence and his sacrifice, and how he approached the last minutes of his life.

Lesson twelve explores Jesus' resurrection and its impact on the lives of Jesus' followers (John 20). You will consider how the resurrection of Jesus sent his followers on a mission.

Lesson thirteen examines our tendency to compare ourselves to other followers of Christ (John 21). It also challenges us to discover our unique calling and ministry.

My prayer for you as you study these lessons is that you will be seized with passion for the kingdom of God and that you will live a victorious life whatever your personal assignment may be in God's story of redemption.[1]

UNIT THREE. JESUS' PASSION AND VICTORY

Lesson 11	"It Is Finished"	John 19:13–30
Lesson 12	"So I Send You"	John 20:1–21
Lesson 13	"What Is That to You?"	John 21:15–23

NOTES

1. Unless otherwise indicated, all Scripture quotations in this unit introduction and lessons 11–13 and the Christmas lesson are from the New International Version. The titles of lessons 11–13 are from the New Revised Standard Version Bible.

Focal Text

John 19:13–30

Background

John 18—19

Main Idea

Jesus completed the work God gave him to do by giving his life on the cross.

Question to Explore

What was "finished" at Golgotha?

Study Aim

To explain the meaning of Jesus' crucifixion and determine how I will respond

Study and Action Emphases

- Affirm the Bible as our authoritative guide for life and ministry
- Share the gospel with all people
- Develop a growing, vibrant faith

LESSON ELEVEN

"It Is Finished"

Quick Read

Jesus completed his mission by giving his life on the cross to defeat Satan's claim on our lives and provide a way for redemption for everyone who believes in him.

The touchdown, the final exam, the end of a project, the dissertation defense, the deal closed, and the final note of the piece prepared for the musical recital all signal the completion of an assignment placed squarely on our shoulders. Few things in life are as gratifying as knowing you have finished something of major significance. Even so, nothing finished can compare with the completion of Jesus' work in the redemption of our lives through his crucifixion.

John 19:13–30

¹³When Pilate heard this, he brought Jesus out and sat down on the judge's seat at a place known as the Stone Pavement (which in Aramaic is Gabbatha). ¹⁴It was the day of Preparation of Passover Week, about the sixth hour.

"Here is your king," Pilate said to the Jews.

¹⁵But they shouted, "Take him away! Take him away! Crucify him!"

"Shall I crucify your king?" Pilate asked.

"We have no king but Caesar," the chief priests answered.

¹⁶Finally Pilate handed him over to them to be crucified.

So the soldiers took charge of Jesus. ¹⁷Carrying his own cross, he went out to the place of the Skull (which in Aramaic is called Golgotha). ¹⁸Here they crucified him, and with him two others—one on each side and Jesus in the middle.

¹⁹Pilate had a notice prepared and fastened to the cross. It read: JESUS OF NAZARETH, THE KING OF THE JEWS. ²⁰Many of the Jews read this sign, for the place where Jesus was crucified was near the city, and the sign was written in Aramaic, Latin and Greek. ²¹The chief priests of the Jews protested to Pilate, "Do not write 'The King of the Jews,' but that this man claimed to be king of the Jews."

²²Pilate answered, "What I have written, I have written."

²³When the soldiers crucified Jesus, they took his clothes, dividing them into four shares, one for each of them, with the undergarment remaining. This garment was seamless, woven in one piece from top to bottom.

²⁴"Let's not tear it," they said to one another. "Let's decide by lot who will get it."

This happened that the scripture might be fulfilled which said,

"They divided my garments among them
and cast lots for my clothing."

So this is what the soldiers did.

²⁵Near the cross of Jesus stood his mother, his mother's sister, Mary the wife of Clopas, and Mary Magdalene. ²⁶When Jesus saw his mother

there, and the disciple whom he loved standing nearby, he said to his mother, "Dear woman, here is your son," **²⁷**and to the disciple, "Here is your mother." From that time on, this disciple took her into his home.

²⁸Later, knowing that all was now completed, and so that the Scripture would be fulfilled, Jesus said, "I am thirsty." **²⁹**A jar of wine vinegar was there, so they soaked a sponge in it, put the sponge on a stalk of the hyssop plant, and lifted it to Jesus' lips. **³⁰**When he had received the drink, Jesus said, "It is finished." With that, he bowed his head and gave up his spirit.

Jesus' Arrest and Trial (18:1—19:12)

The story of Jesus' sacrificial work comes into sharp focus beginning with his arrest in an olive grove (John 18:1–3). On the surface it would seem that Jesus' power was coming to an end. However, even in Jesus' apparent surrender to the authorities, he maintained control of the situation and yielded himself to the work God had assigned him. Jesus' surrender in the olive grove was conditional on the release of his disciples (18:8).

The Gospel of John tells of two sessions of questioning Jesus underwent as a result of his arrest. The first interrogation took place before Annas, the father-in-law of Caiphas, the high priest (18:12–24). Annas then sent him to Caiaphas, who then sent him to Pilate (18:24, 28). The second interrogation took place before Pilate, the Roman governor and highest ranking official in Judea. Pilate, whose official residence was in Caesarea, was the state representative of Rome. Before Pilate, Jesus pointed out that his ministry and teaching was based on the truth (18:29–37). Pilate concluded his interrogation by raising a hypothetical question (18:38): "What is truth?" People still struggle with that question two millennia later.

Finding no fault in Jesus, Pilate was challenged to release Barabbas rather than Jesus (18:39–40). The two sessions of interrogation and the plea to release Barabbas left Pilate with the task of flogging and sentencing Jesus. Yet Pilate could not find a legitimate reason to punish Jesus. The Jewish leaders, though, were determined to have him crucified and pressed Pilate to sentence Jesus (19:1–12).

These events bring us to the part of the crucifixion story where the people demand the death of Jesus. In the midst of these terribly difficult circumstances, Jesus demonstrated an unstoppable focus on the work that his Father sent him to do.

Jesus' Sentence (19:13–16)

The trial of Jesus conducted by Pilate reached its climax when the crowd demanded the death of Jesus, an innocent victim. Pilate found Jesus innocent but was pressed by the threats of Jesus' opponents. He was caught between the proverbial *rock and a hard place.*

> *Jesus managed to maintain focus on his mission right up to the very moment he drew his last breath and gave up his spirit.*

Pilate, as the state representative of the Roman government, ascended his seat at the "Stone Pavement" area to pronounce judgment on Jesus (19:13). The sixth hour of "the day of Preparation," about noon, was when the Passover lamb was slaughtered to begin the celebration of Passover.[1] Passover is the high celebration of Israel's deliverance from slavery in Egypt, in which God demonstrated his power and established himself as King over the people of Israel (see Exodus 12).

Pilate's assertion, "Here is your king," came as a surprise to the Jewish leaders (John 19:14). Pilate was inferring that the only king that the Jewish people would have was Jesus. The Gospel of John records that these insulting words were spoken to "the Jews." In John's Gospel, the Jews were not uniformly opposed to Jesus but are shown to be divided between the uncommitted and the hostile toward Jesus. When "the Jews" are spoken of in a negative manner in the Gospel of John, the term is referring to the Jewish leaders, namely the Pharisees who opposed Jesus rather than the Jewish people as a whole.[2] One of the main goals of John's Gospel is to provide an evangelistic witness so that many will believe (20:30–31) while exposing the emphatic denial of the reality of the gospel message by the Jewish leaders.

Vicious words and verbal insults were not limited to the crowd but found their way into the words of the Roman governor. However, Jesus remained silent and focused on the lives of the men, women, and children for whom he would lay his life down as a ransom and sacrificial gift.

The conclusion of Pilate's pronouncement was that he was handing over Jesus to Jesus' opponents, who would rather crucify an innocent man rather than the guilty man called Barabbas. I am amazed at Jesus' ability to remain silent while others could not keep from spewing out vicious insults.

Are we much different from the people who witnessed the sentencing of Jesus that day? We speak before we think, we aim to hurt with our words, and we seldom consider the impact of our words on the lives of others while pursing our own interests. Silence was Jesus' demonstration of focus on the completion of his task. Proverbs 10:19 says, "When words are many, sin is not absent, but he who holds his tongue is wise." Have you chosen to hold your tongue while fielding false accusations? Have you found silence to be redemptive?

> *Few things in life are as gratifying as knowing you have finished something of major significance.*

Jesus' Sacrifice (19:17–27)

The soldiers took hold of Jesus and assigned him to carry his own cross-beam to Golgotha. There they placed him between two criminals. John describes the place of Jesus' crucifixion not in terms of shame but in terms of prominence. Jesus would be lifted up (see John 3:14; 8:28; 12:32) for all to see.

John's Gospel focuses on several key aspects of Jesus' sacrifice. First, note the title on the cross. It was customary for the one sentenced to

Affecting Others with Your Life

Bill Thornton was my pastor when I came to faith in Jesus Christ. He was the pastor of Memorial Baptist Church in Rialto, California. I was nine years old, and my parents were members of this church. I remember hearing Brother Bill's message one day and coming home to ask my mother, "How can I ask Jesus into my heart and have my sins forgiven?"

My mother shared the gospel with me, and then my parents prayed with me to receive Jesus Christ as my Savior. A year later, Brother Bill baptized me. Years later, I was elected president of the Baptist General Convention of Texas. Brother Bill, who also had moved to Texas, was there to vote for me and share in the blessing and celebration of our Texas Baptist family. His focus on his ministry as a pastor, his willingness to follow Christ, and the dedication of his wife Alta and his children changed my life forever. Whose eternity are you impacting by your obedience to Jesus Christ?

death on a cross to have a placard stating the reason for his execution. Rather than citing Jesus' crime as high treason against the Roman government, Pilate used this opportunity to use the title given to Jesus during his trial: "Jesus of Nazareth, the King of the Jews" (19:19). The placard was written in three languages—Aramaic, the everyday language of the Jews, "that the Jews might understand it"; Latin, the language of Rome, "that the Romans might know it"; and Greek, the most widespread language of the day, "that all nations might learn of it."[3] Pilate, in his attempt to offend the Jewish leaders, became an unknowing announcer of the gospel truth. He who earlier questioned what truth was announced it to those who would witness the crucifixion. Nothing can stop God's redemptive plan in history.

Who are the family and friends who encourage you, support you, and stand by you when you face your greatest challenges?

The second key aspect of the crucifixion dealt with by the Apostle John was division of Jesus' clothes in verses 23–24. According to Roman custom, the clothes of the crucified person became the property of the execution squad. Jesus likely would have been wearing a tunic, an outer garment or robe, sandals, a belt, and a head covering.[4] The soldiers drew straws to win his tunic. The soldiers not only complied with customary Roman practice but also fulfilled prophecy (see Psalm 22:18).

Several loved ones of Jesus were only steps away from this business transaction. Jesus' mother, Mary's sister, Mary the wife of Clopas, and Mary Magdalene witnessed firsthand the death of Jesus. Commentators differ in their views of the number of women present, but it seems as though four women are mentioned here. The first woman was Jesus' mother, Mary. The second woman was Jesus' aunt, Mary's sister. It is possible that she was either Salome, mentioned in Mark 15:40, or the mother of the sons of Zebedee, James and John (Matthew 27:56). This would make James and John cousins of Jesus. The other two women were Mary Magdalene and Mary the wife of Clopas. Who are the family and friends who encourage you, support you, and stand by you when you face your greatest challenges?

Perfect love casts out fear.

A crucified man had the right to make final dispositions and instructions to those who survived him. Jesus, as he focused on his assignment from the Father, took time to look to the interests of others, especially that of his mother. While there are several possible interpretations about "the disciple whom he loved," most commentators agree that the reference was to the Apostle John, author of the Gospel of John, son of Zebedee and Salome, and cousin to Jesus. It makes sense that Jesus would commend his mother into the care of a close relative. Even in his death, Jesus was able to keep focus on his mission and on the care of his mother.

How many times do we lose sight of the family God has entrusted to us while we are busy doing other things, even ministry? The Lord, though, took time for his mother while not losing focus on his primary assignment on the cross. What does it profit us if we gain the whole world and lose those dearest to us?

Jesus' Spirit (19:28–30)

Jesus managed to maintain focus on his mission right up to the very moment he drew his last breath and gave up his spirit. The Gospel of John records that while Jesus was dying on the cross he uttered two sentences.

The first sentence Jesus spoke was, "I am thirsty" (19:28). A hyssop branch soaked in vinegar was given to him. Exodus 12:22 describes the hyssop branch being used to spread blood from the slain lamb over the doorpost of the Israelite homes when the angel of death passed by at the time of the Exodus. The reference may seem somewhat remote, but it is still useful in understanding the significance of this scene.

Nothing can stop God's redemptive plan in history.

The last sentence Jesus said before he died was, "It is finished" (19:30). The word in the Greek language is *tetelestai*, signifying full completion. Jesus voluntarily surrendered his life to the purpose God had set before him. He finished it and released his spirit. His focus on doing his mission was so acute that he had the presence of mind to confess that his work was done just before he drew his last breath.

Joseph of Arimathea was prepared to ask Pilate for Jesus' body to bury him (19:38). He was a rich man (Matt. 27:57), an important member of the Sanhedrin (Mark 15:43; Luke 23:50). He apparently was both a good and righteous man (Luke 23:50) and a person who lived with the expectation of God fulfilling the promise of the coming of the kingdom (Mark 15:43; Luke 23:51). He was a disciple of Jesus but kept this fact confidential for fear of reprisal. Since the Roman tradition added to the shame of

Application Thoughts

- One way to apply this lesson to your life is to seek to discover your own life's mission. What is the reason you are living? What results are worth your life? Can you write these thoughts in a sentence?
- Do you have a friend who is going through a tough time? How can you help? This will require your availability and time. Pray and ask the Lord to put someone on your mind in your circle of influence who needs a friend.
- Begin praying for God to provide you opportunities to make new friends for Christ. Look for ways to ask questions in a conversational format with a friend that will lead to questions about faith. Seek to learn and understand before telling.

---

crucifixion the refusal to allow a decent burial, Joseph's efforts to provide Jesus with a decent burial stand out. Jewish tradition did not allow for crucified criminals to be buried with the bodies of other family members or in family tombs for fear of contaminating those already buried there. Burial sites for crucified Jews were reserved in a section away from the city.

What does it profit us if we gain the whole world and lose those dearest to us?

Joseph's action was courageous since he was not even a family member of Jesus. His position and wealth may have made a difference. The fact that Pilate agreed to release the body to Joseph supports the idea that Pilate did not really support the charges brought against Jesus. Pilate released Jesus' lifeless body to Joseph for burial.

Nicodemus also accompanied Joseph in the burial process. This same Nicodemus had approached Jesus at night in John 3. These two disciples worked together. Joseph provided the grave, and Nicodemus provided the spices for burial. These men should have feared for their lives, but they courageously took action to care for Jesus after his death. Perfect love casts out fear.

QUESTIONS

1. Why was it important for Jesus to complete his mission on the cross?

2. Who are the friends and family you can count on when you are experiencing your most difficult day?

3. How are you combining care for your family with your life mission and purpose?

4. What opportunities do you have to reveal publicly that you are a follower of Jesus Christ? Would those around you be surprised?

5. What is the meaning of Jesus' crucifixion for you?

NOTES

1. George Beasley-Murray, *John*, Word Biblical Commentary, Volume 36 (Waco, Texas: Word Books, Publisher, 1987), 341.
2. Beasley-Murray, *John*, lxxxix.
3. Beasley-Murray, *John*, 346.
4. Beasley-Murray, *John*, 347.

Focal Text
John 20:1–21

Background
John 20

Main Idea
Jesus' resurrection validates his identity and his mission and calls us to participate with him in that mission.

Question to Explore
Where is the risen Jesus sending you?

Study Aim
To lead the class to affirm the meaning of Jesus' resurrection for their lives and decide how they will respond to Jesus' sending them on his mission

Study and Action Emphases

- Affirm the Bible as our authoritative guide for life and ministry
- Share the gospel with all people
- Develop a growing, vibrant faith
- Include all God's family in decision-making and service
- Value all people as created in the image of God

LESSON TWELVE

"So I Send You"

Quick Read
Authentic personal knowledge of the reality of Jesus' resurrection generates a course in the life of Jesus' followers toward advancing the mission of God.

Were it not for the fact that Jesus carried out his plans and demonstrated the reality of his resurrection to his followers, the resurrection would still seem unreal. Jesus does what he says he will do even if it is unbelievable from our perspective.

The reality of the resurrection is still a source of debate for many unbelieving people in the world around us. The reality of the resurrection even seemed unbelievable to the followers of Jesus. Nevertheless, the Gospel of John reports the events of the resurrection as fact, reality, and truth.

John 20:1–21

[1]Early on the first day of the week, while it was still dark, Mary Magdalene went to the tomb and saw that the stone had been removed from the entrance. [2]So she came running to Simon Peter and the other disciple, the one Jesus loved, and said, "They have taken the Lord out of the tomb, and we don't know where they have put him!"

[3]So Peter and the other disciple started for the tomb. [4]Both were running, but the other disciple outran Peter and reached the tomb first. [5]He bent over and looked in at the strips of linen lying there but did not go in. [6]Then Simon Peter, who was behind him, arrived and went into the tomb. He saw the strips of linen lying there, [7]as well as the burial cloth that had been around Jesus' head. The cloth was folded up by itself, separate from the linen. [8]Finally the other disciple, who had reached the tomb first, also went inside. He saw and believed. [9](They still did not understand from Scripture that Jesus had to rise from the dead.)

[10]Then the disciples went back to their homes, [11]but Mary stood outside the tomb crying. As she wept, she bent over to look into the tomb [12]and saw two angels in white, seated where Jesus' body had been, one at the head and the other at the foot.

[13]They asked her, "Woman, why are you crying?"

"They have taken my Lord away," she said, "and I don't know where they have put him." [14]At this, she turned around and saw Jesus standing there, but she did not realize that it was Jesus.

[15]"Woman," he said, "why are you crying? Who is it you are looking for?"

Thinking he was the gardener, she said, "Sir, if you have carried him away, tell me where you have put him, and I will get him."

[16]Jesus said to her, "Mary."

She turned toward him and cried out in Aramaic, "Rabboni!" (which means Teacher).

> **17**Jesus said, "Do not hold on to me, for I have not yet returned to the Father. Go instead to my brothers and tell them, 'I am returning to my Father and your Father, to my God and your God.'"
>
> **18**Mary Magdalene went to the disciples with the news: "I have seen the Lord!" And she told them that he had said these things to her.
>
> **19**On the evening of that first day of the week, when the disciples were together, with the doors locked for fear of the Jews, Jesus came and stood among them and said, "Peace be with you!" **20**After he said this, he showed them his hands and side. The disciples were overjoyed when they saw the Lord.
>
> **21**Again Jesus said, "Peace be with you! As the Father has sent me, I am sending you."

Unbelievable Experience: The Empty Tomb (20:1–9)

The Gospel of John is careful to describe the circumstances Mary Magdalene experienced when she arrived at Jesus' tomb. She found that the stone had been rolled away from the entrance. This fact was enough to send Mary Magdalene running toward Peter and one of the other disciples, "the one Jesus loved" (John 20:2).

Mary Magdalene was from the village of Magdala, on the western shore of the Sea

Jesus does what he says he will do even if it is unbelievable from our perspective.

of Galilee, and she had followed Jesus from Galilee to Jerusalem. Mary Magdalene's running indicates that a powerful emotion was activated in her. Perhaps it was fear, joy, or excitement.

Whatever the case with Mary Magdalene, upon hearing the news of the empty tomb, Peter and the unidentified disciple also began running. "The other disciple" beat Peter to the tomb (20:4). In first-century Jewish culture, the testimony provided by a woman was not considered credible. Appropriate and credible testimony could be established by two Jewish males, hence the appearing of Peter and the other disciple. The identity of "the other disciple, the one Jesus loved" (20:2) is not specified, but the traditional identification is that he was the Apostle John (see 11:3; 13:23; 19:26–27; 21:7, 20–25).

Another indicator of the reality of Jesus' resurrection is the reference to Jesus' grave clothes. The "other disciple" discovered the grave clothes, strips of linen, lying in the grave in addition to the burial cloth that had been around Jesus' head. The Gospel writer reports that "the burial cloth that had been around Jesus' head" was separate from the linen and was folded up by itself. This account is in stark contrast to the burial clothes wrapped around Lazarus when Jesus called him out of the grave (11:44). Lazarus rose from the dead by the power of Jesus' voice but came out of the tomb wrapped in his grave clothes. Jesus, on the other hand, rose from the dead and left the clothes behind, intact.

The rolled-away stone, the empty tomb, and the burial clothes left behind pointed to one thing: Jesus was alive. Even so, "they still did not understand from Scripture that Jesus had to rise from the dead" (20:9).

Unbelievable Reality: The Resurrected Lord (20:10–18)

The disciples returned to their homes, but Mary could not shake the experience of finding the empty tomb. She was overcome emotionally. She then looked into the tomb again, only to see two angels dressed in white. They were sitting where Jesus' body had been. The angels quizzed her as to the nature of her tears. She responded with the impression that someone had stolen her Lord's body.

Mary immediately turned away. She saw Jesus but did not recognize him. Jesus asked her again about her tears and then asked (20:15), "Who is it you are looking for?" Mary mistook Jesus for the gardener. Mary did not notice anything different about the appearance of Jesus that would distinguish him from the average person. Too, at that point, Mary was focused on the goal of recovering Jesus' body and placing it in an appropriate grave.

What is the future that Jesus is sending you to work toward?

Jesus turned to Mary and addressed her directly. The moment Jesus called her name, "Mary," she immediately knew it was the Lord. She cried out to him (20:16), "Rabboni!" The Gospel of John explains that "Rabboni" means "Teacher." The word translated "Rabboni" is used only in this verse and in Mark 10:51.

It is interesting to note the various transformative experiences after the resurrection in which disciples recognized that Jesus had been resurrected. In this case, the transformative moment was evoked by one word, Mary's name (20:16). In the Emmaus story in Luke 24:13–35, the transformative moment came when the resurrected Lord broke bread. "Then their eyes were opened and they recognized him" (Luke 24:31). For Peter and others, it was the appearance of Jesus (Luke 24:34; John 20:19–20). What is it about the resurrected Lord that calls you to respond to his presence in your life? Is it the way Jesus calls your name? Is it the way you see Jesus work through your church and in the lives of people?

Jesus is always sending us on a personal mission, a personal assignment, to proclaim his reign and rule and to invite others to participate in it.

Jesus responded to Mary by saying, "Do not hold on to me, for I have not returned to the Father." Jesus was saying, *Cease clinging to me.* The time for experiencing Jesus through touching and clinging had passed because Jesus was making the transition between resurrection and ascension. The Gospel of John seems to combine the resurrection and the ascension into one event even though Luke in his Gospel and in Acts (Luke 24:50–53; Acts 1:6–11) reports these events as distinct and separate. Jesus was at the tomb only because he had not gone back to the Father. So the point of Jesus' saying, *Cease clinging to me,* was not that Jesus' body was not tangible but that he was on his way to the Father. Mary's experience underscores the physical reality of the resurrection. John in 1 John 1:1 also makes clear that the witnesses of Jesus heard him, saw him, and touched him.

After telling Mary not to "hold on to me" (John 20:17), the Lord gave Mary instructions to find the other disciples and to tell them that he was on his way back to the Father.

Missions and You

1. Consider writing out a mission statement for your life. In other words, what do you want to be remembered for? Use this statement to make decisions for how you will serve the Lord.
2. Consider gathering your family and doing the same thing with them.
3. Consider a family mission trip to another country or in a cross-cultural context. For help in finding a place to serve, contact Worldconnex at www.worldconnex.org.
4. Work with your church's missions committee to start a new congregation among a cultural group different from those attending your church.

Mary was so moved by this experience that she felt compelled to find the disciples immediately to tell them everything she experienced. When she found the disciples, she summed up her experience by saying (20:18), "I have seen the Lord!" Mary's exclamation was another piece of evidence that the Lord had arisen. The "other disciple" had seen the empty tomb and believed (20:8).

Mary's report was not believed, however, and was regarded "like nonsense," according to Luke 24:11. The Lord would need to deal with the disciples directly.

We are not much unlike Mary in that we tend to gravitate to clinging to Jesus rather than to telling others of what we have experienced with Jesus. We tend to lean toward staying with the Lord rather than going on the mission to which Jesus has called us. What is the future that Jesus is sending you to work toward? Jesus is always sending us on a personal mission, a personal assignment, to proclaim his reign and rule and to invite others to participate in it.

Unbelievable Responsibility: Mission of a Lifetime (20:19–21)

The mission of the disciples came into sharper focus when Jesus, in his resurrection body, came into the locked room where the disciples were meeting. They were there behind locked doors because they feared that a detachment of guards would come to seize them. Jesus came and stood right in the middle of the meeting and said (20:19), "Peace be with you!"

> It is hard to believe that Jesus has entrusted his mission to us and that our life's mission could be connected to the mission of Christ in the world.

This type of greeting was a common Eastern salutation given upon entering a room. Other than that, nothing about the experience was ordinary.

Do you ever find yourself living on the wrong side of the resurrection, in hiding, in fear, perhaps even in hiding on the inside of the church, seeking protection there? This is where the disciples were at this point in the story. They were in hiding, in fear, and in the comfort of a makeshift sanctuary when the Lord appeared to them.

Jesus immediately "showed them his hands and side" (20:20). The disciples were "overjoyed" when they saw their Lord again.

After more than thirty years of preaching the gospel, the best cure I have ever experienced for fear is the very presence of Jesus in my life. When I get connected to Jesus in a personal way, I am ready to go out from where I am. His presence produces my joy. When Jesus comes and speaks "peace" to me, I have the peace that passes all understanding and a new joy that gets me back on mission for him.

The disciples were overjoyed because they saw Jesus. The wounds in Jesus' hands and in his side were the evidence of a victorious Lord. Peace and joy filled the private gathering of the disciples.

Jesus then repeated his original greeting (20:19, 21), "Peace be with you!" Perhaps Jesus repeated this greeting to reassure his disciples of his real presence and to set the context for his commission to them (see also Matthew 28:16–20; Luke 24:46–49; Acts 1:3–11). Jesus said, "As the Father has sent me, I am sending you." Jesus was challenging his disciples to give their lives in service (John 13:15), to do greater works than he had done (14:12), and to testify of him (15:27). The mission of Jesus was to continue through the hands of the disciples. This commission would not be limited to the disciples in the room but was intended for all the followers of Jesus. The mission of Jesus would now be the shared responsibility of the followers of Jesus.

> *The mission of Jesus was to continue through the hands of the disciples.*

It is hard to believe that Jesus has entrusted his mission to us and that our life's mission could be connected to the mission of Christ in the world. It is an unbelievable responsibility that results in a mission for a lifetime. This mission is not simply delegated to us but is shared with us and empowered by the Holy Spirit. Jesus turned to his disciples, "breathed on them, and said, 'Receive the Holy Spirit'" (20:22). He commended to them the ministry of announcing the terms of forgiveness.

The disciples found Thomas and told him they had seen the Lord. Thomas, though, required proof. "A week later his disciples were in the house again, and Thomas was with them" (20:26). Although the doors were locked, Jesus appeared before them once again. He used the same greeting (20:26), "Peace be with you!" Then Jesus addressed Thomas directly and asked him to put his finger on the hands and the side of Jesus. Jesus invited Thomas to believe. Thomas confessed (20:28), "My Lord and my God!" Jesus commended Thomas for his belief as well as those who would not have the privilege of seeing but would believe.

John closed out this part of the resurrection story by indicating that Jesus did many other miraculous signs that were not recorded in his Gospel. He emphasized that what had been written was written so that we "may believe that Jesus is the Christ . . . and have life in his name" (20:31). John concluded that what he had written was sufficient for future readers to believe on the name of Jesus and find life.

> *The reality of the resurrection has the potential of igniting our lives with passion and faith.*

Jesus' disciples responded with deep emotion and energy when faced with the reality of the resurrection. Their passionate response was to see and believe. Can you remember a time when you saw God at work with your very eyes? Have you seen Jesus transform a person's life? Has Jesus visited your life in unbelievable ways?

Our response is to see and believe. The reality of the resurrection has the potential of igniting our lives with passion and faith. As you review the reality of the panorama of God's work in your life, does the view build passionate faith in you?

We have not seen Jesus in his bodily form, but we have the written record of these unbelievable events. Too, we have become Jesus' body, and we have received the Holy Spirit. Will you become part of the band of followers of Jesus who take seriously the mission to share the good news, to be Jesus' body and presence to a world that needs him? It is the mission of a lifetime. Where is the resurrected Lord sending you in your community, country, or world?

QUESTIONS

1. What evidence can you point to in your life that validates the reality of the resurrection of Jesus Christ?

2. If someone was to describe the passion of your life, the thing most important to you, what would it be?

3. If you were to sum up your life's mission in one sentence, what would you say?

4. How are you participating in pursuing the mission of Jesus on earth?

Focal Text
John 21:15–23

Background
John 21

Main Idea
Our responsibility is to follow Jesus by serving him in our own unique way.

Question to Explore
Why do people—even Christians—sometimes compare themselves to others rather than living their own unique lives?

Study Aim
To commit myself to filling my unique role of service rather than comparing myself to others

Study and Action Emphases

- Affirm the Bible as our authoritative guide for life and ministry
- Share the gospel with all people
- Develop a growing, vibrant faith
- Obey and serve Jesus by meeting physical, spiritual, and emotional needs
- Equip people for servant leadership

LESSON THIRTEEN "What Is That to You?"

Quick Read
Authentic followers of Jesus Christ willingly affirm their unique role as servants of Christ and embrace their personal assignments to advance the kingdom of God.

My calling to serve as president of Hispanic Baptist Theological Seminary (now Baptist University of the Americas) in 1999 magnified my experience of accepting God's assignment for my life. I had been serving as founding pastor of Pueblo Nuevo Community Church in El Paso for the previous seven years of my ministry. I was committed to living out the rest of my ministry in El Paso rather than looking for greener pastures. I was fully immersed in my ministry and not interested in another location.

One day, a call came from the chair of the presidential search committee for Hispanic Baptist Theological Seminary. He advised me that the committee was interested in interviewing me. I agreed to participate in the process, thinking that there was no real possibility that I would be selected. I thought that it would be good to go through the process to possibly influence the future of the seminary, even indirectly. I went to the first interview prepared to share from my heart and speak of the potential of the school. I shared my vision for what could happen at the school. Then I returned to El Paso convinced that I would not hear from the committee again.

I was totally surprised when the chair of the search committee called me again to indicate that I was the candidate the committee settled on. I was invited for a second interview and about a week later received a third call indicating that the committee voted to extend a call to me to serve as the next president of Hispanic Baptist Theological Seminary. I asked for a week to pray about this decision and to discuss it with my family. I came to the end of the week still looking for answers.

Every person in my circle of influence, including my wife, agreed that the seminary would be an ideal fit for me and for the school. I was uncertain, though. I was so focused on my current ministry that I was unwilling to consider seriously that the Master of life was calling me to another assignment. I searched the Scriptures, prayed, and reflected into the early morning hours before the day that I was to give my answer. When I finally realized that I was the only person blocking the obvious call on my life and that I was only a servant and not the Master, I confessed this to the Lord and went to bed.

The next morning I shared the experience with my wife Belinda and then called the chair of the search committee. On July 22, 1999, the Board of Trustees of the seminary unanimously voted to extend a call to me to serve as the sixth president. I began my new assignment on August 1, 1999, and I continue to serve in this unique place of ministry.

The challenge of every believer is to find his or her unique expression as a servant in response to the resurrected Master. This challenge was faced by the first disciples of Christ and resonates with those of us who follow him today. The background for this story begins in John 21 with the description of Thomas, Peter, Nathanael, the sons of Zebedee, and two other disciples on their way back to fishing. They had just seen the resurrected Jesus and had decided to go back to their former way of life in the fishing business. They had fished all night and caught nothing. Jesus, who was standing on the shore, called out to the disciples to cast their nets to the other side. They did as Jesus instructed, even though they did not recognize Jesus. As a result, they could not retrieve the nets full of fish.

At this point, one of the disciples said, "It is the Lord!" (John 21:7). They immediately went to shore to meet Jesus. They found Jesus by "a fire of burning coals," preparing breakfast (21:9). This was now the third appearance of Jesus to his disciples (21:14). The Gospel of John underscores the reality and humanity of the resurrected Lord with this reference to Jesus preparing and eating breakfast with his disciples.

Too, even in Jesus' post-resurrection state, he served his followers. Serving others is a hallmark of the life Jesus' disciples were and are to lead. Do you see yourself as a servant? What are the characteristics that mark us as authentic servants of the risen Lord? What does it take to make a servant after the pattern of Jesus?

John 21:15–23

¹⁵When they had finished eating, Jesus said to Simon Peter, "Simon son of John, do you truly love me more than these?"

"Yes, Lord," he said, "you know that I love you."

Jesus said, "Feed my lambs."

¹⁶Again Jesus said, "Simon son of John, do you truly love me?"

He answered, "Yes, Lord, you know that I love you."

Jesus said, "Take care of my sheep."

¹⁷The third time he said to him, "Simon son of John, do you love me?" Peter was hurt because Jesus asked him the third time, "Do you love me?" He said, "Lord, you know all things; you know that I love you."

Jesus said, "Feed my sheep. ¹⁸I tell you the truth, when you were younger you dressed yourself and went where you wanted; but when you are old you will stretch out your hands, and someone else will dress you and lead you where you do not want to go." ¹⁹Jesus said this to indicate the kind of death by which Peter would glorify God. Then he said to him, "Follow me!"

20Peter turned and saw that the disciple whom Jesus loved was following them. (This was the one who had leaned back against Jesus at the supper and had said, "Lord, who is going to betray you?") **21**When Peter saw him, he asked, "Lord, what about him?"

22Jesus answered, "If I want him to remain alive until I return, what is that to you? You must follow me." **23**Because of this, the rumor spread among the brothers that this disciple would not die. But Jesus did not say that he would not die; he only said, "If I want him to remain alive until I return, what is that to you?"

The Making of a Servant: Humility, Restoration, and Mission (21:15–19)

What could have been going through the minds of Peter, Thomas, Nathanael, and the other disciples during their breakfast with Jesus? Would they have been reminded of how Jesus fed the five thousand with bread and fish (John 6)? Would they have remembered the first words of Jesus' invitation to follow them: "From now on you will catch men" (Luke 5:10)? Would they have remembered how Jesus washed their feet (John 13)? Now Jesus was serving them breakfast.

Following breakfast Jesus engaged Peter in restorative conversation. Jesus initiated a conversation to get to the heart of the matter. Peter previously had denied Jesus three times (John 18:15–27). Perhaps Jesus pulled Peter aside to deal with him personally. Jesus asked him (21:15), "Do you truly love me more than these?"

Perhaps Jesus questioned Peter three times to get to the deep recesses of Peter's heart regarding potential service. Jesus was securing the humility needed from Peter for service.

What did Jesus mean by "more than these" (21:15)? Perhaps Jesus was asking Peter whether he loved Jesus more than the fish, the fishing business, or anything else that would stand in the way of authentic service. Perhaps "these" referred to the other disciples. In other words, did Peter love Jesus more than Peter loved the other disciples? Or did Peter love Jesus more than the other disciples loved Jesus? My view is that the reference is the first choice. That is, did Peter love Jesus more than he loved the things in his life, such as fishing or the fishing business? This is the crux of servanthood: to love the Master more than anything and more than life itself.

Humility is an act of submission. Was Peter willing to submit to the absolute will of the Master? Finding one's humility is part of the restoration process. When we find humility in our hearts toward the Master, we are restored into a proper relationship with him.

Jesus' questioning Peter in this way—asking a similar question three times—seems highly unusual. Perhaps Jesus was not satisfied with Peter's answers and so Jesus asked again and again. Perhaps, too, Jesus' three questions point to the ancient custom of making an affirmative declaration three times in public in order for it to have contractual or legal viability. Whatever the case, Jesus seems to have used this conversation with Peter to re-establish and restore Peter as the leader Jesus intended him to be.

Do you see yourself as a servant?

Another interesting feature of this redemptive and restorative conversation is Jesus' use of the word "love" when Jesus asked (John 21:15, 16), "Do you truly love me?" The first two times Jesus asked Peter whether Peter loved him Jesus used a form of the word *agapao*, the strong word for *love* that appears in John 3:16. *Agapao* commonly is transliterated into English as *agape*. It is the word denoting divine love and usually carries the meaning of will or purpose as well as affection. On the other hand, the word Jesus used in the third question was a form of the Greek word *phileo*, meaning *affinity, fondness,* and *friendship*. It suggests a lesser kind of love. Jesus evidently was seeking to get Peter to evaluate the kind of love for him that he truly had.

Note the variations in Jesus' responses to Peter, too. In the first and third responses, Jesus instructed Peter to "feed" his "lambs" or "sheep" (21:15, 17). The second time, though, Jesus instructed Peter to "take care

A Shepherding Challenge

Many Hispanic youth drop out of high school before finishing. What would happen if the Baptist churches in your association or state committed to take a zero-tolerance posture for the Hispanic dropout rate? What if we were to focus primarily on the Hispanic youth in our Hispanic Baptist congregations? What if Baptists gained the reputation of ensuring all Baptist youth received a high school education?

of" his sheep. Jesus not only intended taking the sheep to pasture but also included a full guardianship of the sheep.

In verses 18 and 19, Jesus changed the subject to look ahead at the kind of sacrifice Peter would be making when Peter committed himself to the mission assigned to him. He was looking ahead to the kind of death Peter would face. Jesus was the Good Shepherd and laid his life down for his sheep (10:15). In a similar way, Peter would also have to come to the point of laying down his life for the sheep Jesus was entrusting to him (21:19).

What are the characteristics that mark us as authentic servants of the risen Lord?

Jesus closed this subject by saying (21:19), "Follow me!" The verb translated "follow" is present imperative and thus literally means *keep on following me*. The invitation by Jesus to follow him may lead us to lay down our lives for his sake. That is, in fact, what we do when we live our lives each day. We give up or use up our hours for Jesus' sake and Jesus' purpose. But for some, this following may include what might be considered a premature death. We all have an appointment with death some day. So we should ask ourselves, *To what are we giving our lives prior to that appointment? For what reason do we live? To what purpose will we die?*

The Making of a Servant: Clarity and Calling (21:20–23)

Peter had just received a personal commission from the risen Lord but could not help but notice that "the disciple whom Jesus loved" was following close behind. Many commentators say that this disciple was John. However, he is not named specifically. Peter might have been curious or uneasy about this disciple's role in the future. Peter stopped to ask (21:21),

What does it take to make a servant after the pattern of Jesus?

"What about him?" The question was out of place. The risen Lord had dealt directly with Peter in his conversation of restoration. Only moments later, Peter wanted to focus on the destiny of the disciple Jesus loved. Jesus focuses on us, and yet we tend to focus on comparisons with others. What is it about us that we are not satisfied with Jesus' focus on our lives and we must look to the lives of others?

Jesus' response was swift and to the point. He challenged Peter (21:22), "If I want him to remain alive until I return, what is that to you?" The

Finding Your Place to Serve

1. Gather your family and ask them to inventory the unique qualities the family has and then reflect on how God could uniquely use your family to bless other families.
2. Consider tithing a portion of your time to explore ways you can minister to the poorest and most disadvantaged people in your city.
3. Lead your church missions committee to identify in a Hispanic mission in your area one or two Hispanic youth you would be willing to mentor, tutor, and encourage to finish high school and go to college.

phrase "until I return" was cause for some controversy related to Jesus' return and the end of time. There was an expectation in John's writings that Jesus' return was imminent. Perhaps the disciples believed that Jesus was to return before the last of the living disciples passed away. This thought was quite appealing in light of the eschatological hope of the early church.

Jesus' response was a sharp rebuke to Peter! In essence, Jesus was saying, *Don't be concerned about the other disciple or his future. Rather, focus on your continued effort to follow me.* A rumor spread that the disciple Jesus mentioned was not going to die, but the gospel writer was careful to clarify that this was not what Jesus, in fact, said. Rumors get started by folks hearing what they want to hear, misunderstanding what has been said, misquoting what was said, or inventing what was said and passing it on. The solution is

> *This is the crux of servanthood: to love the Master more than anything and more than life itself.*

to go back to the source and get clarification. That is exactly what the Gospel writer did. The goal of this passage of Scripture was to clarify the focus of Peter on his own mission assignment and to call him to follow. The making of a servant leader requires clarity and calling.

The Making of a Servant: Authenticity and Imagination (21:24–25)

The closing verses of the Gospel of John affirm the authenticity of what the writer has just recorded and the authenticity of the writer himself. It appears that the one who wrote the Gospel is "the disciple whom Jesus loved." The next sentence, "We know that this testimony is true," may indicate a narrator in addition to the writer of the Gospel. Perhaps "we" refers to the elders of the church at Ephesus, to the author of the Gospel, to the author of the Gospel and others closely associated with him, or to the author and the church to which he belonged.

Jesus focuses on us, and yet we tend to focus on comparisons with others.

The point of the "we" is to demonstrate that a community of believers was willing to authenticate what had been written.

John closed out his narration by admitting that there were many other things that Jesus did that were not recorded and could not be contained in any number of volumes of books. It appears that John was suggesting that even though only a fraction of what Jesus did was captured in his Gospel, it remains one of the most valuable assets the church possesses. John used his imagination to consider what it would take to capture in literary form all that Jesus did in his ministry. The gospel is authentic, and its potential for impacting lives cannot be contained in our imagination.

QUESTIONS

1. What is the unique role or assignment of your life?

2. What does this incident suggest about relating to a fellow believer who has failed to demonstrate a pattern of living for the resurrected Lord?

3. What is the best remedy against the temptation to compare ourselves and our mission assignments to that of other Christians?

4. What would folks say about our authenticity and imagination as living testaments of the risen Lord?

Focal Text
Matthew 2:1–12

Background
Matthew 1:18—2:23

Main Idea
The Christ child attracts people the world over.

Question to Explore
What will happen after Christmas?

Study Aim
To decide on at least one way I will share Christ with all the world after Christmas

Study and Action Emphases

- Affirm the Bible as our authoritative guide for life and ministry
- Share the gospel with all people
- Develop a growing, vibrant faith
- Value all people as created in the image of God
- Encourage healthy families
- Obey and serve Jesus by meeting physical, spiritual, and emotional needs

CHRISTMAS LESSON After Jesus Was Born

Quick Read
Authentic followers of Jesus Christ willingly give their lives to implement God's plan to share the good news message of Jesus Christ with people of all nations and all languages on all continents of the world.

Visionary leaders who speak prophetically to the church suggest that the twenty-first century will mirror the first century in many ways. We have a reasonable amount of global peace, similar in some ways to the *Pax Romana* of the first century. We have a widespread common language, English, similar to the widespread use of Greek in the first century. Too, in the first century, Roman roads enabled global commerce; in the twenty-first century, we have the internet and air travel.

Philip Jenkins in his book *The Next Christendom* suggests that Christianity in the twenty-first century will have come full circle. He suggests that by 2050 the center of gravity of Christianity will have shifted firmly to the southern half of the globe. He also affirms that by 2050 only one in five Christians worldwide will be non-Latino white. Eighty percent of Christians will hail from Latin America, Asia, and Africa.[1]

We are also in the midst of a movement of global migration. The East is coming to the West, and the South is coming to the North to intersect in the United States of America. Hispanic people are flowing into the agricultural South, Midwest, and as far as Alaska in the United States and also to Canada. Demographers who study Texas suggest that by the year 2015, every other Texan will be Hispanic.

Population changes also will reflect dramatic growth among African and Asian populations in the United States. More than 175 languages are spoken in the United States today.

We are living in one of the most expansive mission fields the world has ever known. Mission possibilities have come to our doorsteps. Our challenge is no longer to cross the seas, although that effort is still needed. Our real challenge is much closer. Our challenge is about crossing the street. Our mission frontiers will not require passports and plane tickets to cross geographic boundaries. Our new frontiers are cross-cultural rather than cross-continental. How will we take the good news message of Jesus in this dramatically different context?

The Christmas story is a personal story of one family working through the experience of a supernatural birth and the coming of the Messiah as a child. Matthew's goal in his Gospel was to develop a picture of the Messiah in the context of a kingly heritage. Jesus was to be the coming Messiah of the Jews. This Messiah would come to live among the people, show them the face of God, and then die for them in their place.

The events that led to Jesus were unusual. Mary was pregnant, but without having had sexual relationships. Joseph, her husband, was overwhelmed by the experience of an angel speaking to him to affirm God's work in his family. All of these things were in place to fulfill what was recorded in Scripture by the prophet who said, "'The virgin will be with child and will give birth to a son, and they will call him Immanuel'—which means, 'God with us'" (Matthew 1:23; see Isaiah 7:14). Joseph and Mary could be assured that God would be with them in the experiences they were about to go through.

Matthew 2:1–12

¹After Jesus was born in Bethlehem in Judea, during the time of King Herod, Magi from the east came to Jerusalem ²and asked, "Where is the one who has been born king of the Jews? We saw his star in the east and have come to worship him."

³When King Herod heard this he was disturbed, and all Jerusalem with him. ⁴When he had called together all the people's chief priests and teachers of the law, he asked them where the Christ was to be born. ⁵"In Bethlehem in Judea," they replied, "for this is what the prophet has written:

⁶ "'But you, Bethlehem, in the land of Judah,
are by no means least among the rulers of Judah;
for out of you will come a ruler
who will be the shepherd of my people Israel.'"

⁷Then Herod called the Magi secretly and found out from them the exact time the star had appeared. ⁸He sent them to Bethlehem and said, "Go and make a careful search for the child. As soon as you find him, report to me, so that I too may go and worship him."

⁹After they had heard the king, they went on their way, and the star they had seen in the east went ahead of them until it stopped over the place where the child was. ¹⁰When they saw the star, they were overjoyed. ¹¹On coming to the house, they saw the child with his mother Mary, and they bowed down and worshiped him. Then they opened their treasures and presented him with gifts of gold and of incense and of myrrh. ¹²And having been warned in a dream not to go back to Herod, they returned to their country by another route.

The Far East to Bethlehem (2:1–2)

Matthew's purpose was to describe how the Messianic King was received as a newborn. It is a tale of contrasts. Homage was paid from afar, but the

Child experienced rejection in his own country. Mary and Joseph traveled to Bethlehem, the place near where Jacob buried Rachel (Genesis 35:19) and Ruth met Boaz (Ruth 1:22—2:6), because it was the original family home for both of them.

Wise Men from the East came to worship Jesus. "Magi" is a transliteration of the Greek word often translated "Wise Men." In New Testament times Magi referred to a wide variety of people interested in dreams, astrology, magic, and books thought to contain mysterious references to the future. "Magi" is the origin of our word *magician*. Matthew points out the astrological interest of the Magi who came to find the newborn "king of the Jews" (Matt. 2:2). Since Babylon was the origin of astrology, it is possible to think of these Magi originating from Babylon, Persia, or other places in that region, or perhaps Arabia. We are not sure that there were three Magi since there is no mention as to the number of Magi who came to worship Jesus. We know only that they brought three gifts. The word translated "east" is *anatolon*, which means *from the rising of the sun*.

> *Visionary leaders who speak prophetically to the church suggest that the twenty-first century will mirror the first century in many ways.*

Ministering to Hispanics

Baptist University of the Americas (BUA) will observe its sixtieth anniversary in 2007 and will celebrate this milestone with students from more than fifteen different countries speaking at least five languages. In 1947 Baptist University of the Americas (BUA) began as the Mexican Baptist Bible Institute. It was designed to prepare pastors for Spanish-speaking populations in Texas. Later the school became Hispanic Baptist Theological Seminary (HBTS). Over time the school focused on the preparation of bilingual and bicultural ministers. In 2003 HBTS became Baptist University of the Americas, reflecting a predominantly Hispanic student body (ninety percent) as well as Anglo, African, and Asian-American students.

BUA seeks to bridge cultures and build lives for Texas and the world. Missiologists contend that the people group most effective at sharing the good news with Arabs will come from the Hispanic community. Hispanics and Arabs share common history, language, culture, and physical similarities. What will be your part to ensure that Hispanics are called, equipped, and sent to the world far and near?

Matthew has documented that the first gift-bearing worshipers of Jesus were not Jews but Gentiles from the East. The prophet Isaiah had pointed to the coming of a king who would judge between the nations and settle disputes for many peoples. Nations would cease to take up a sword against other nations (Isaiah 2:2–4). John's Gospel records Jesus saying, "But I, when I am lifted up from the earth, will draw all men to me" (John 12:32). Jesus would later command his followers to make disciples of all nations (Matt. 28:19–20). Matthew's attention on the details of the visit of the Magi serves to foreshadow the global nature of the good news.

Mission possibilities have come to our doorsteps.

The Magi came asking (2:2), "Where is the one who has been born king of the Jews?" The question raised by the Magi posed a problem for Herod. Herod had not been "born king." On the other had, Jesus had indeed been "born king." Jesus was of the lineage of the great King David, as Matthew had established in the genealogy in Matthew 1. Herod was the usurper of the throne if Jesus had been "born king of the Jews."

The Magi went on to say that they spotted the star of Jesus "in the east" (2:2). That does not mean they saw the star positioned in the east. They would have gone east to follow it. The phrase "in the east" means they were in the East when they saw the star, or *we saw his star at its rising*.

These men might have been Jewish prose-lytes and might have known of the Messianic hope. Whatever the case, Jesus was "born king of the Jews." This irreversible, incontrovertible fact set the course of history. Gentiles from the East came searching for this king. The same kind of longing resides in the hearts of women and men all over the world, who come from everywhere to find the Prince of Peace. They search for the King of heaven. What is our role in helping them find the King?

Power, might, and prestige . . . were no match for God's plans to redeem the world through the Christ child.

A Disturbance in the King's Court (2:3–8)

King Herod "was disturbed" by the question of the Magi. "Disturbed" refers to *being in turmoil* or *greatly agitated*. Herod was not the only person "disturbed" by the question of the Magi. Included in "all Jerusalem with him" being disturbed were the Pharisees and Sadducees.

Herod convened a group of religious leaders, "all the people's chief priests and teachers of the law," to inquire where Jesus was to be born (Matt. 2:4). The answer to the question of "where the Christ was to be born" came from Micah 5:2. In the verse is found the shepherding imagery that Jesus used often. Hebrews 13:20 calls Jesus the "great shepherd." Jesus called himself "the good shepherd" (John 10:11). Jesus told Peter to "take care of my sheep" (John 21:16). Peter called Christ "the shepherd" (1 Peter 2:25), and John's Revelation refers to Jesus as the "shepherd" (Revelation 7:17). The shepherd imagery appears often in the Old Testament (Ezekiel 34) and implies guidance, pastoral care, and compassion. Jesus would rule over the people but would also shepherd them. Jesus is the shepherd of my soul and my life. Has there been a time in your life when you needed the Lord to care for your soul?

This passage reminds us . . . that the gospel is not just for our family.

Herod's next move was to gather the Magi, after he learned from the religious leaders about the Christ child (Matt. 2:7). Herod had no intentions of worshiping Jesus. He developed a creative lie to engage the Christ seekers from the East. Herod's instructions to the Magi were that they "make a careful search for the child" (2:8) and then bring Herod word of his location.

Herod was so sure of his success that he did not even send an escort with the Magi. Herod was hoping to gain their trust and confidence in the process. Power, might, and prestige, though, were no match for God's plans to redeem the world through the Christ child. Indeed, nothing can stop God's purpose and plan in redemption history. God will carry out his purposes without fail. The ruler of the world could not stop the Savior of the world (John 3:16; 4:42; 12:32). God intervened in the Christmas story to ensure that Jesus would be protected and the Gentile worshipers would carry news of what they found and what they experienced.

From Bethlehem to the Far East (2:9–12)

The Magi left Herod's courts and followed the star to the place where Jesus was born. This is the first time that the star was said to have moved, guiding the Magi to the place of Jesus' birth. The motion of the star at

Things to Do After Christmas

1. Read *Ministering Cross Culturally: An Incarnational Approach to Relationships* by Sherwood Lingenfelter and Marvin K. Mayers, and reflect on your cross-cultural competence for the world that is streaming towards us.

2. Read *Cross-Cultural Conflict* by Duane Elmer to learn about non-Western approaches to resolving conflict with biblical authenticity and relational integrity among people whose culture is different from yours.

3. Consider learning Spanish in order to minister more effectively to Hispanics. You could enroll, for example, in an Immersion Class through the Center for Cultural and Language Studies at Baptist University of the Americas to learn conversational Spanish and cross-cultural competency in the Hispanic context. (See www.bua.edu for more information or call 800-721-1396, extension 208).

---

this point in the story was a supernatural event. Matthew records that "when they saw the star, they were overjoyed" (Matt. 2:10). Their joy was due to the success of their search.

"On coming to the house, they saw the child with his mother Mary, and they bowed down and worshiped him" (2:11). The beginning of the story of Christ's birth has a global and multinational texture. So does the final chapter of history, when people from every tribe and tongue will gather around the throne to worship the Lamb of God (Revelation 7:9–10).

After the Magi worshiped Jesus, the Child, they presented him with gifts. The custom of bringing gifts was important in the ancient East when appearing before a superior (Genesis 43:11; 1 Samuel 9:7–8; 1 Kings 10:2). Frankincense is a glittering, odorous gum obtained by making incisions in the bark of several trees. Myrrh was considered a highly valued perfume, and spice was used in embalming. Some commentators have suggested the symbolic meaning of these gifts. The gold was to suggest royalty,

. . . The gospel is for everyone.

incense was to suggest divinity, and myrrh was to suggest the passion and burial of Christ. Other authors suggest that such speculation is overdone. Rather, these gifts were simply expensive gifts.

Matthew closed out this part of the story by highlighting God's intervention. The Lord warned the Magi through a dream that they should not go back to Herod. So they returned to their country by another route. The worshipers left Bethlehem and went to the East with treasure in their hearts.

Conclusion

God chose to break into our small-mindedness and provincialism through a family gathered around a manger. God came to this family, and he comes to our families, to transform us and send us out into the world on mission for the Christ child.

Authentic followers of Jesus Christ willingly give their lives to implement God's plan to share the good news of Jesus Christ with people of all nations and all languages on all continents of the world.

Christmas is one of the high celebration times of the year for families. People want to be with their families during this season to celebrate the coming of Jesus into the world through a family. Our family gatherings at Christmas represent another opportunity to reflect on the difference Jesus has made in children, parents, and families in the past year.

This passage reminds us, though, that the gospel is not just for our family. Rather, the gospel is for everyone. Authentic followers of Jesus Christ willingly give their lives to implement God's plan to share the good news of Jesus Christ with people of all nations and all languages on all continents of the world.

QUESTIONS

1. What are the implications of the Christmas story with its transnational texture—Magi coming from the Gentile world to see the infant King?

2. What does the coming of the Gentile, pagan, Magi from the East to find Jesus at his birth say to us concerning people who come to the United States seeking a better life and answers to their spiritual questions?

3. Do you struggle with issues of power, control, jealousy, and rage during the Christmas season, or are your thoughts filled with exceeding joy and peace during the season when we celebrate Jesus' birth?

4. What will the Christmas story this year impress you to do regarding the poor, the foreigner, the imprisoned, the oppressed, and the physically limited people in your community?

5. After the presents are opened, the wrapping paper stuffed into the trash bags, and the tree is removed, what difference will celebrating Christmas make in your life on January 1? What will change about you this year to reflect the impact of Jesus on your life?

NOTES

1. Philip Jenkins, *The Next Christendom: The Coming of Global Christianity* (New York: Oxford University Press, 2002).

THE BOOK OF ACTS: *Toward Being a Missional Church*

Additional Resources for Studying the Book of Acts[1]

F. F. Bruce. *The Book of the Acts*. The New International Commentary on the New Testament. Grand Rapids, Michigan: Eerdmans, 1988.

Richard N. Longenecker. "Acts." *The Expositor's Bible Commentary*. Grand Rapids, Michigan: Zondervan, 1981.

J. W. MacGorman. *Acts: The Gospel for All People*. Nashville, Tennessee: Convention Press, 1990.

Howard Marshall. *Acts*. Tyndale New Testament Commentaries. Grand Rapids, Michigan: Eerdmans, 1980.

John B. Polhill. *Acts*. The New American Commentary. Volume 26. Nashville, Tennessee: Broadman Press, 1992.

A. T. Robertson. *Word Pictures in the New Testament*. Volume III. Nashville, Tennessee: Broadman Press, 1930.

T.C. Smith. *Acts*. The Broadman Bible Commentary. Volume 10. Nashville, Tennessee: Broadman Press, 1970.

Frank Stagg. *The Book of Acts: The Early Struggle for an Unhindered Gospel*. Nashville, Tennessee: Broadman Press, 1955.

John R. W. Stott. *The Message of Acts*. The Bible Speaks Today. Downers Grove, Illinois: InterVarsity, 1994.

William H. Willimon. *Acts*. Interpretation: A Bible Commentary for Teaching and Preaching. Atlanta: John Knox Press, 1988.

NOTES

1. Listing a book does not imply full agreement by the writers or BAPTISTWAY PRESS® with all of its comments.

How to Order More Bible Study Materials

It's easy! Just fill in the following information. For additional Bible study materials, see www.baptistwaypress.org or get a complete order form of available materials by calling 1–866–249–1799 or e-mailing baptistway@bgct.org.

Title of item	Price	Quantity	Cost
This Issue:			
The Gospel of John: The Word Became Flesh—Study Guide	$2.75	_____	_____
The Gospel of John: The Word Became Flesh—Large Print Study Guide	$2.85	_____	_____
The Gospel of John: The Word Became Flesh—Teaching Guide	$3.25	_____	_____
Additional Issues Available:			
Genesis 12–50: Family Matters—Study Guide	$1.95	_____	_____
Genesis 12–50: Family Matters—Large Print Study Guide	$1.95	_____	_____
Genesis 12–50: Family Matters—Teaching Guide	$2.45	_____	_____
Exodus: Freed to Follow God—Study Guide	$2.35	_____	_____
Exodus: Freed to Follow God—Large Print Study Guide	$2.35	_____	_____
Exodus: Freed to Follow God—Teaching Guide	$2.95	_____	_____
Leviticus, Numbers, Deuteronomy—Study Guide	$2.35	_____	_____
Leviticus, Numbers, Deuteronomy—Large Print Study Guide	$2.35	_____	_____
Leviticus, Numbers, Deuteronomy—Teaching Guide	$2.95	_____	_____
Joshua and Judges—Study Guide	$2.35	_____	_____
Joshua and Judges—Large Print Study Guide	$2.35	_____	_____
Joshua and Judges—Teaching Guide	$2.95	_____	_____
1 and 2 Samuel—Study Guide	$2.35	_____	_____
1 and 2 Samuel—Large Print Study Guide	$2.35	_____	_____
1 and 2 Samuel—Teaching Guide	$2.95	_____	_____
Psalms and Proverbs: Songs and Sayings of Faith—Study Guide	$2.75	_____	_____
Psalms and Proverbs: Songs and Sayings of Faith—Large Print Study Guide	$2.85	_____	_____
Psalms and Proverbs: Songs and Sayings of Faith—Teaching Guide	$3.25	_____	_____
Matthew: Jesus' Teachings—Study Guide	$2.35	_____	_____
Matthew: Jesus' Teachings—Large Print Study Guide	$2.35	_____	_____
Matthew: Jesus' Teachings—Teaching Guide	$2.95	_____	_____
Jesus in the Gospel of Mark—Study Guide	$1.95	_____	_____
Jesus in the Gospel of Mark—Large Print Study Guide	$1.95	_____	_____
Jesus in the Gospel of Mark—Teaching Guide	$2.45	_____	_____
Luke: Journeying to the Cross—Study Guide	$2.35	_____	_____
Luke: Journeying to the Cross—Large Print Study Guide	$2.35	_____	_____
Luke: Journeying to the Cross—Teaching Guide	$2.95	_____	_____
1 Corinthians—Study Guide	$1.95	_____	_____
1 Corinthians—Teaching Guide	$2.45	_____	_____
2 Corinthians: Taking Ministry Personally—Study Guide	$2.35	_____	_____
2 Corinthians: Taking Ministry Personally—Large Print Study Guide	$2.35	_____	_____
2 Corinthians: Taking Ministry Personally—Teaching Guide	$2.95	_____	_____
1, 2 Timothy, Titus, Philemon—Study Guide	$2.75	_____	_____
1, 2 Timothy, Titus, Philemon—Large Print Study Guide	$2.85	_____	_____
1, 2 Timothy, Titus, Philemon—Teaching Guide	$3.25	_____	_____
Hebrews and James—Study Guide	$1.95	_____	_____
Hebrews and James—Teaching Guide	$2.45	_____	_____
Revelation—Study Guide	$2.35	_____	_____
Revelation—Large Print Study Guide	$2.35	_____	_____
Revelation—Teaching Guide	$2.95	_____	_____

Coming for use beginning March 2007

Acts: Toward Being a Missional Church—Study Guide	$2.75	
Acts: Toward Being a Missional Church—Large Print Study Guide	$2.85	
Acts: Toward Being a Missional Church—Teaching Guide	$3.25	

Baptist Doctrine and Heritage

The Bible—You Can Believe It	$4.95	
The Bible—You Can Believe It—Teaching Guide	$1.95	

Beliefs Important to Baptists

Beliefs Important to Baptists—Study Guide (one-volume edition; includes all lessons)	$2.35	
Beliefs Important to Baptists—Teaching Guide (one-volume edition; includes all lessons)	$1.95	
Who in the World Are Baptists, Anyway? (one lesson)	$ .45	
Who in the World Are Baptists, Anyway?—Teacher's Edition	$ .55	
Beliefs Important to Baptists: I (four lessons)	$1.35	
Beliefs Important to Baptists: I—Teacher's Edition	$1.75	
Beliefs Important to Baptists: II (four lessons)	$1.35	
Beliefs Important to Baptists: II—Teacher's Edition	$1.75	
Beliefs Important to Baptists: III (four lessons)	$1.35	
Beliefs Important to Baptists: III—Teacher's Edition	$1.75	

For Children

Let's Explore Baptist Beliefs	$ 3.95	
Let's Explore Baptist Beliefs—Leader's Guide	$ 2.95	

Cost of Items*

*Shipping and handling charges as well as applicable taxes will be added.
Please call 1–866–249–1799 if the exact amount is needed prior to ordering

Please allow three weeks for standard delivery. For express shipping service: Call 1–866–249–1799 for information on additional charges.

YOUR NAME   PHONE

YOUR CHURCH   DATE ORDERED

MAILING ADDRESS

CITY   STATE   ZIP CODE

MAIL this form with your check for the total amount to
BAPTISTWAY PRESS, Baptist General Convention of Texas,
333 North Washington, Dallas, TX 75246–1798
(Make checks to "Baptist Executive Board.")

OR, **FAX** your order anytime to: 214-828-5376, and we will bill you.

OR, **CALL** your order toll-free: 1–866–249–1799
(M–Th 8:30 a.m.-8:30 p.m.; Fri 8:30 a.m.-5:00 p.m.),
and we will bill you.

OR, **E-MAIL** your order to our internet e-mail address: baptistway@bgct.org,
and we will bill you.

OR, **ORDER ONLINE** at www.baptistwaypress.org.

We look forward to receiving your order! Thank you!